Instructional Assessment of English Language Learners in the K–8 Classroom

DIANE K. BRANTLEY

California State University, San Bernardino

PEARSON

Boston   New York   San Francisco
Mexico City   Montreal   Toronto   London   Madrid   Munich   Paris
Hong Kong   Singapore   Tokyo   Cape Town   Sydney

Executive Editor: *Aurora Martínez Ramos*
Series Editorial Assistant: *Lynda Giles*
Executive Marketing Manager: *Krista Clark*
Production Editor: *Paula Carroll*
Editorial Production Service: *Publishers' Design and Production Services, Inc.*
Composition Buyer: *Linda Cox*
Manufacturing Buyer: *Linda Morris*
Electronic Composition: *Publishers' Design and Production Services, Inc.*
Cover Administrator: *Linda Knowles*

For related titles and support materials, visit our online catalog at www.ablongman.com.

Between the time website information is gathered and then published, it is not unusual for some sites to have closed. Also, the transcription of URLs can result in typographical errors. The publisher would appreciate notification where these errors occur so that they may be corrected in subsequent editions.

CIP data unavailable at press time.
ISBN 0-205-45599-9

Printed in the United States of America

10 9 8 7 6 5 4 3   10

Photo credits: All photos in the book were supplied by Nathaniel Wildes, Tactical Graphics.

*To my mother Nora,
who showed me the joy
of reading, writing, and
creative storytelling . . .*

Contents

CHAPTER FIVE

Reading Acquisition in the Primary and Secondary Languages 59

CHAPTER SIX

Assessment and Development of Concepts of Print, Phonemic Awareness, and the Alphabetic Principle 77

CHAPTER SEVEN

Assessment and Development of Word Identification, Comprehension, and Reading Fluency 95

CHAPTER EIGHT

Assessment and Development of Written Language and Spelling   111

CHAPTER NINE

Assessment in the Content Areas   127

CHAPTER TEN

Putting the Pieces Together   137

CHAPTER ELEVEN

Instructional Assessment in Practice: A Case Study   151

APPENDICES

Preface

This book will provide classroom teachers in grades K–8 with specific assessments that can be administered to English Language Learners (ELLs) within the regular classroom. The assessments will cover a range of literacy skills deemed necessary for English language acquisition and reproduction, while also assessing the students' literacy skills in their primary languages. Additionally, each chapter contains instructional strategies to provide teachers with a resource for preparing meaningful, assessment-based instruction for ELLs.

This text will allow teachers to acquire a deep understanding of the value of instructional assessment for ELLs and the importance of evaluating the results to provide the students with immediate, appropriate, and meaningful instruction within the regular classroom setting. While the main emphasis is on the second language learner, teachers will find that many of the assessments can also be utilized with English-only students as well.

Rationale for Writing the Text

The primary rationale for writing a book such as this rests on the realization that classroom teachers have few resources available to them to assess ELLs within their classrooms. Most texts focus on English-only students with little emphasis on those students whose primary language is not English. When ELLs are mentioned, it is often in a short paragraph at the end of a chapter or as an aside. With the ever-changing demographics of schools across the nation, it is inappropriate to overlook or marginalize such a large segment of the school population and leave teachers unequipped to meet the needs of all of their students. We are long overdue for a book whose primary focus is on the needs of our second language students within the classroom.

Features of the Text

This book contains a variety of textual features that will improve the reader's understanding of the content under study. These features are predicated on research-based strategies that are known to increase reading comprehension. Several features of the text include:

1. *Anticipation Guides:* Each chapter begins with an anticipation guide (Readence, Bean, & Baldwin, 1998) that requires readers to use their background knowledge to either agree or disagree with the information presented. The guide allows readers to engage in a cognitive discussion with the author prior to reading the chapter. It is a strategy that helps readers to set a purpose for reading and then to read on to confirm or disprove their initial responses. The anticipation guide will be revisited at the conclusion of each chapter.

2. *Vignettes:* Embedded within most chapters are short vignettes that focus on a particular academic or social issue related to the content of the chapter. The vignettes are based on real-life teaching situations and serve to engage the reader in the authentic application of the assessments and strategies within any given chapter.

3. *Highlighted Assessment Vocabulary:* Within each chapter, important vocabulary will be highlighted within the written text. By drawing attention to specific assessment and instructional vocabulary, the reader gains an appreciation of the importance of learning key vocabulary words necessary for understanding the content presented within the chapter. The highlighted vocabulary is specific to assessment and instruction and will be useful to the reader in day-to-day educational contexts.

4. *Effective Research-Based Teaching Practices:* Each chapter containing a language arts–specific domain has a section dedicated to providing the reader with detailed information regarding specific learning strategies that are beneficial to second language learners. These strategies are particular to the concepts under study within the chapter.

5. *Assessment Toolkit:* Because each chapter focuses on an explicit facet of second language assessment and acquisition, it is imperative to have a section that details all of the materials needed to assess ELLs within the classroom. These materials can be put into a "kit" that will be easily accessible to the teacher as needed. This is a practical and necessary component of developing a sound assessment and evaluation system for the classroom.

6. *Revisiting the Chapter Anticipation Guide:* Each chapter ends with a brief overview of the main points of the content presented in the initial anticipation guide. This allows readers to check their understanding of what they've read by comparing it to the culminating information at the end of the chapter. It also serves to summarize the concepts under study.

Each of the textual features discussed above serves to make the information presented comprehensible and practical to the classroom teacher. It will provide a quick reference guide for use at the beginning and ending of a school year, while also serving those students who enter the classroom once the school year has begun.

Organization of the Text

This book is organized to support the reader in the process of developing a rich understanding of the special instructional needs of ELLs within the regular classroom. To do so, first it is necessary to develop an awareness and true understanding of the cultures and home literacies of today's ELLs. This is essential in order to provide ELLs with a classroom environment that is warm and welcoming. Second, it is important to understand the various theories of second language acquisition and the programs that have been developed to enhance English acquisition in schools across the nation. Third, it is useful to develop a common language in regard to the instructional and theoretical foundations of assessment and evaluation before delving into the specifics of the various categories of assessment available to classroom teachers. Next, the text will address the specific areas of language arts related to the development, acquisition, and reproduction of the English language. These areas are: (a) oral language development and vocabulary, (b) concepts of print and the alphabetic principle, (c) word recognition and word identification strategies, (d) reading fluency, (e) reading comprehension, (f) written language development and spelling, and (g) content area literacy.

The book presents a section devoted to maintaining an ongoing assessment, evaluation, and instructional program that allows teachers to develop a picture of the whole student, identifying both strengths and areas of need. It also details various methods for communicating with parents that encourage teachers to form an educational collaboration with them in order to support the students' continued academic success. The book concludes with a case study that allows the reader to apply the knowledge gleaned from previous chapters in a user-friendly format that supports the connected nature of assessment and instruction.

On a more personal note, it is my belief that our second language students bring a wealth of knowledge to our classrooms that is often left untapped. By accurately assessing and evaluating our ELLs, we will be better able to reach them and help them to become bicultural, biliterate members of our diverse school system. The goal is not to marginalize these students, but to allow them to have access to the opportunities afforded to the English-speaking population in our classrooms.

Acknowledgments

First, I want to share my gratitude for my husband, Charles Brantley, who patiently nudged me to write draft after draft of my first book. I also want to thank my mentor and colleague, Nancy P. Gallavan, for her guidance and inspiration over the years as I completed my doctorate, and later, this book.

I am also grateful to the teachers and graduate students I have worked with during the past five years for providing me with their personal teaching experiences and insights, especially my niece, Shawn Gibson Dean. I especially appreciate the feedback from the reviewers as well: Stephanie Dhonau, University of Arkansas at Little Rock; Randi Freeman, Central Washington University; and Diane Taboada, Stanford University. Also, I want to thank Aurora Martínez Ramos for believing in me as I wrote this book.

Finally, I want to thank Nathaniel Wildes for photographing the students and teachers who appear throughout the text, for without them, none of this would have been possible.

CHAPTER ONE

English Language Learners in Today's K–8 Classrooms

READ THROUGH EACH of the following statements in the table prior to reading the chapter. Place a checkmark in either the box labeled "agree" or "disagree," depending upon whether you believe the statement to be true or false. As you read the chapter, refer back to the chart and confirm or modify your initial responses.

Initial Chapter Anticipation Guide

Agree	Disagree	Statement
		Approximately 10 percent of all teachers in the United States have students in their classrooms who are English Language Learners (ELLs).
		Many teachers feel unequipped to meet the needs of their ELLs.
		Culture is an inherited set of qualities each person brings to school.
		In order to better understand ELLs, it is important for teachers to understand their own cultures.
		Teachers can act as cultural mediators through the use of multicultural literature, varying participatory structures, and styles of classroom management.

The statements presented in the anticipation guide serve as a great starting point for our conversation about culture and the role of teachers within our linguistically and culturally diverse classrooms. Read on to find out the actual experiences of a novice teacher as she begins her first day of school. As you are reading through the vignette, think about your own early teaching experiences.

TEACHER *VIGNETTE*

When I walked into my second-grade classroom on the first day of school, I saw a room filled with faces from across the globe. Though it seemed as if everyone spoke English, as I listened more carefully, I could hear an abundance of Spanish being spoken throughout the room. Having lived in California all of my life, I was accustomed to seeing and hearing a variety of languages, but not being biliterate myself, I felt unequipped to teach my Spanish-speaking students. A sense of panic swept over me as I began to teach on that very first day of school.

Author, 1987

The story told above is one that is experienced by many first-year teachers across the nation. While this may be the case, it was not comforting to me as I stood in front of my first class of students, fresh out of my teacher credentialing program. I received a solid education but somehow was unequipped to address the needs of the diverse population of my second-grade classroom. My sole desire was to provide my students with a wonderful second-grade experience filled with rich reading and writing activities. I wanted the students to gain a love of reading and show tremendous growth in all academic areas. When I walked into my classroom, I was afraid that I would let my students down because of my lack of knowledge and experience. It was this fear that led me to learn how to be an effective teacher of first and second language students. My goal now is to share some of what I have learned over the past eighteen years as an educator.

Who Are Today's English Language Learners?

It has been several years since I first stepped into a classroom, and many changes have taken place during that time period. As of the year 2000, the United States population was comprised of 11.1 percent non-native born residents. This equates to more than 31.1 million people who have immigrated to the United States, up more than 57 percent from the year 1990 (U.S. Census Bureau, 2000). Of the U.S. population, 214,809,283 people speak only English. Another 48 million residents speak languages other than English. Of these 48 million people, close to 30 million speak Spanish, approximately 10 million speak various Indo-European languages, 7.5 million speak

Asian and Pacific Island languages, and close to 2 million people speak a variety of other languages (U.S. Census Bureau, 2000). With such linguistic and cultural diversity in our country and an increased demand for standardization of the curriculum, we face a variety of challenges within our school system.

In a recent survey of approximately 3 million U.S. teachers conducted by the National Center for Educational Statistics, 41 percent stated that they teach students with limited English proficiency (LEP), while fewer than 12.5 percent reported having special ELL training of over eight hours in duration. This statistic supports the premise that teachers feel ill-equipped to meet the special needs of their linguistically diverse students. In fact, Zhao (2002) asserts that there "is only one qualified teacher available for every 100 ELLs" (p. A1). Unfortunately, this also demonstrates that little has changed for teachers since I began teaching almost two decades ago.

So what can teachers do to make a change for the better within their own classrooms? First, it is important to get to know your school's population in order to provide all students with a safe environment in which to learn. Next, teachers can specifically target the students in their own classrooms as they seek to gain a deeper understanding of the cultures of their students. By educating ourselves about our school population, we have taken a major step toward ensuring the success of our ELLs.

Today's classrooms are comprised of students from varying cultural and linguistc backgrounds. Unfortunately, many teachers feel unprepared to meet the special needs of this more diverse population.

Understanding Culture and Home Literacy

All students who enter our classrooms bring with them rich cultural histories, social discourses, and multiple literacies that contribute to and enhance the makeup of our schools. Whether they are native speakers of English or another language, it is imperative that teachers become familiar with their students' backgrounds in order to better understand their feelings, strengths, needs, and interests. This knowledge helps teachers to provide more meaningful learning experiences for students, which in turn leads to a greater chance of academic success.

Peregoy and Boyle (2001) suggest gathering some basic information about each student when he or she arrives at school. First, they recommend asking several essential questions:

- What country is the student from?
- How long has the student lived in the United States?
- Where does the student live and who are the members of the family living in the home?
- What languages are spoken at home?
- Under what circumstances did the family move to the United States?
- What are the student's previous educational experiences? (pp. 4-5).

By asking these questions, teachers will garner valuable information that can be used to make the student's transition into the new environment much easier. It will also allow the teacher to make appropriate educational decisions for the student, supporting his or her journey into learning to speak, read, and write in a new language while simultaneously supporting the home language and culture. It is imperative that the child feels that his or her home language is valued and supported throughout the process of acquiring fluency in English. Keeping this in mind, how can teachers support the acquisition of a second language within the classroom and value the child's home culture and literacy?

ENCULTURATION:
"Enculturation is the process of acquiring the characteristics of a given culture and generally becoming competent in its language and ways of behaving and knowing" (Gollnick & Chinn, 2002, p. 7).

Creating a Welcoming Classroom Culture

Culture is a construct that is all encompassing. It is defined as the "knowledge, beliefs, arts, morals, law, custom, and any other capabilities and habits acquired by man (sic) as a member of society" (Scupin, 2000, p. 6). Therefore, it involves everything that makes us who we are, and it makes us both unique and also a member of a group. Culture is not inherited but rather learned through a process termed **enculturation**.

Enculturation occurs on two levels: consciously, as the child is taught appropriate behaviors by those closest to him or her growing up, and unconsciously, through the social interactions, experiences, texts, and observations taking place on a daily basis.

Creating a welcoming classroom culture therefore involves an understanding of the child's home culture while introducing the nuances of the school and, in particular, the classroom. As much as possible, it becomes important to ensure that the two cultures are compatible as a means of providing the child with a safe and positive environment in which to learn. This can be done in a variety of ways that will be discussed throughout the remainder of this chapter.

Developing an Intercultural Orientation

Teachers can begin to create a welcoming environment by developing an **intercultural orientation**. This is described in Bennett and Bennett's (1996) Model of Intercultural Sensitivity as a move away from viewing one's own culture as the measure by which all others are judged. Instead, teachers develop empathy and cultural sensitivity, allowing them to see the world through multiple lenses (Díaz-Rico & Weed, 2002). One of the first steps in this process is for teachers to understand their own cultures and how they enhance or interfere with their ability to teach their students. By better understanding ourselves, we are often better able to understand others.

The Aspects of Culture Questionnaire (Table 1.1), provides a series of questions aimed at developing a deeper understanding of culture. It is based on the works of Kottler and Kottler (2002), Peregoy and Boyle (2001), Scupin (2000), and Saville-Troike (1978). It would be beneficial to think about the nine aspects of culture presented in the table in regard to your own home culture prior to considering the culture of your students.

INTERCULTURAL ORIENTATION:
A belief system in which a teacher is culturally sensitive to and knowledgeable about cultures other than his or her own. This awareness allows a teacher to understand the world from multiple perspectives without valuing one culture over another (Bennett & Bennett, 1996; Díaz-Rico & Weed, 2002).

By developing an intercultural orientation, a teacher is more likely to meet the needs of all students, regardless of linguistic and cultural background. When problems occur in schools between students and teachers of varying cultures, these problems can often be traced back to misunderstandings that developed early on because of cultural differences. For example, a teacher might have a classroom environment in which the students are placed in cooperative groups and are asked to collaborate on various activities each day. Within this structure, students are encouraged to collaboratively solve a math problem or talk about an issue and then share their responses with the rest of the class. Divergent thinking is promoted and valued. For students coming from cultures in which the teacher is seen as the "holder of the knowledge" and a lecture format is

TABLE 1.1   Aspects of Culture Questionnaire

Aspects of Culture	*Questions*
Configuration of the Family/ Family Roles	What is the hierarchical structure of the family? How is family defined? What are the roles of the various family members? How does gender impact the role/status of the family members?
Languages and Social Discourses of the Culture	What is the primary language spoken at home? How do people greet each other? What are the primary and secondary discourses used in the culture? How do people take turns? How do people show they are paying attention?
Family Traditions and Celebrations	What holidays and celebrations are customary? Are these public and/or private celebrations? What rituals and traditions exist within the culture?
Religious Beliefs and Affiliations	What religious beliefs are held by the family? Are there any specific restrictions and public rituals associated with the religion?
Home Literacy Practices	What are the home literacy traditions experienced by the family? Are they oral and/or written? What types of books, folktales, and music are customary? In what ways are the home literacy practices compatible with and different from school literacy practices?
Educational Beliefs/Practices	What are the student's previous educational experiences? What is the role of the teacher and the family in education? What type of educational support is provided in the home? Who provides this support?
Social Norms of the Culture	What are considered to be appropriate behaviors for children when at school? Is punctuality valued within the culture? What behaviors are socially acceptable for boys and girls? Do they differ?
Food, Clothing, Music, and Cultural Artifacts	What traditional foods are eaten at home? Are there any dietary restrictions? What is the customary style of dress within the culture? What symbols and artifacts are important within the culture?
Discipline and Authority	Who is responsible for disciplining the child? What is deemed as appropriate discipline? What rules of behavior are essential within the culture? Who is the authority figure within the home? How should discipline issues be handled at school?

Source: Information taken from Kottler & Kottler (2002), Peregoy & Boyle (2001), Scupin (2000), and Saville-Troike (1978).

Teachers can act as cultural mediators for ELLS by familiarizing themselves with their students' backgrounds. This information helps to create a warm and welcoming environment for students.

CULTURAL MEDIATORS:
Teachers and other educational professionals who promote culturally responsive teaching practices, classroom groupings, response strategies, and classroom materials that provide students with a safe and welcoming classroom environment (Diaz & Flores, 2001).

the appropriate form of teaching, this type of classroom can be quite unsettling for students and their parents. This type of participatory educational structure may cause the parents to question the skills of the teacher and the quality of education at the school site when in fact it is a misunderstanding based on culturally based differences regarding educational beliefs, social norms, and authority. If a teacher is aware of these differences ahead of time and spends time communicating with parents about the reasons for integrating cooperative activities into the curriculum, many of these misunderstandings can be prevented.

It is through this knowledge that teachers can act as **cultural mediators** (Diaz & Flores, 2001) who are able to find the appropriate books, activities, participation structures, and classroom management systems best suited for the students.

ACADEMIC DISIDENTIFICATION:
A process by which students disconnect from the educational system because of a feeling that they are not valued or supported by their teachers, counselors, peers, and/or other educational personnel (Osbourne, 1997).

Teachers as Cultural Mediators

Teachers are often the most important link between the home and the school for students. Students who feel alienated from school because of a belief that their home culture and language are not valued often develop feelings of isolation and **academic disidentification** (Osbourne, 1997). By acting as cultural mediators, teachers can decrease this level of dissonance and encourage students to become actively involved in the classroom. This can be done in a variety of ways, but one of the most natural ways is by reading aloud books from various cultures to the entire class using an interactive strategy the promotes critical discussion of the texts. Building upon the scenario previously presented in which problems grew because of a misunderstanding in the educational structures used in the classroom, teachers can address a variety of cultural differences using a book such as Gary Soto's *Pacific Crossing* (1992). In this book, two Latino boys from San Francisco travel to Japan as a part of an exchange program for students studying the martial art of kempo. While in Japan, they stay at the homes of two different Japanese host families. As you can imagine, many interesting and enlightening conversations take place regarding cultural differences and similarities between the teenaged boys. Additionally, more serious conversations occur between the boys and their host parents, some centering around historical events taking place during World War II. By grounding these serious issues in a fictional story, teachers and students can initially talk about cultural differences in a safe context and then transfer their discussions to events in their own lives. Literature becomes a means to initiate these powerful conversations and eliminate cultural misunderstandings while developing a sense of community among the members of the classroom.

Table 1.2 provides a list of books and authors that is reflective of the rich multicultural literature available to teachers. While the list is just a sampling of what is available, it does provide an idea of the types of books that can be used to enhance the learning experience for all students.

By integrating a variety of books into the daily classroom curriculum, students begin to feel a sense of belonging and ownership within the classroom culture. They see cultural models and soon realize that they are a valued part of the classroom community.

Building upon the use of multicultural literature and developing a safe, welcoming learning environment is the need to create a curriculum that is reflective of the strengths and needs the students bring to school. At the foundation of this is the creation of an assessment and instruction model that is flexible and cognizant of how children learn. In the next section, I will make visible a theoretical framework for assessment and instruction that values students while also helping them to achieve academic success.

TABLE 1.2   Multicultural Literature

Author & Publication Year	Title	Publisher/Age Level	Culture
Bruchac, J. (1992)	*American Indian Animal Stories*	Fulcrum Publishers, Ages: 11–13	Native American
Cheng, A. (2000)	*Grandfather Counts*	Lee & Low Publishers, Ages: 5–8	Asian Pacific Islander
Cisneros, S. (1994)	*Hairs/Pelitos*	Knopf Publishers, Ages: 5–8	Latino
Cisneros, S. (1991)	*The House on Mango Street*	Vintage Publishers, Ages: 11–13	Latino
Curtis, C.P. (1999)	*Bud, Not Buddy*	Delacorte Publishers, Ages: 11–13	African American
Delacre, L. (1996)	*Golden Tales: Myths, Legends, and Folktales from Latin America***	Scholastic Publishers, Ages: 8–10	Latino
Harjo, J. (2000)	*The Good Luck Cat*	Harcourt Publishers, Ages: 5–8	Native American
Hausherr, R. (1997)	*Celebrating Families*	Scholastic Publishers, Ages: 5–8	Multicultural/ Multiethnic
Ho, M. (1996)	*Maples in the Mist: Poems for Children from the Tang Dynasty*	Lothrop Publishers, Ages: 8–10	Asian Pacific Islander
King, C. & Osborne, L.B. (1997)	*Oh, Freedom! Kids Talk About the Civil Rights Movement with the People Who Made It Happen*	Knopf Publishers, Ages: 11–13	Multiethnic/ Multicultural
McKissack, P. (1988)	*Mirandy and Brother Wind*	Knopf Publishers, Ages: 5–8	African American
Reiser, L. (1993)	*Margaret and Margarita/Margarita y Margaret*	Greenwillow Publishers, Ages: 2–5	Latino
Ryan, P.M. (2000)	*Esperanza Rising***	Scholastic Publishers, Ages: 11–13	Latino
Soto, G. (1992)	*Pacific Crossing*	Harcourt Books, Ages: 11-13	Asian Latino

(Continued)

TABLE 1.2   *(Continued)*

Author & Publication Year	Title	Publisher/Age Level	Culture
Thong, R. (2000)	*Round Is a Mooncake: A Book of Shapes*	Chronicle Publishers, Ages: 2–5	Asian Pacific Islander
Van Camp, R. (1998)	*What's the Most Beautiful Thing You Know About Horses?*	Children's Book Press, Ages: 8–10	Native American
Walter, M.P. (1998)	*Justin and the Best Biscuits in the World*	Lothrop Publishers, Ages: 8–10	African American
Weiss, G.D. & Thiele, B. (1995)	*What a Wonderful World*	Antheneum Publishers, Ages: 2–5	Multicultural/ Multiethnic
Wheeler, B. (1986)	*Where Did You Get Your Moccasins?*	Peguis Publishers, Ages: 2–5	Native American
Yep, L. (1989)	*The Rainbow People*	Harper Collins Publishers, Ages: 11–13	Asian Pacific Islander
Zolotow, C. (2000)	*Do You Know What I'll Do?*	Harper Collins Publishers, Ages: 2–5	African American

** Available in other language/s

Foundations of Assessing and Instructing English Language Learners within the Classroom Context

> **What a child can do in cooperation today, he [sic] can do alone tomorrow.**   (Vygotsky, 1962, p. 104)

SOCIOCULTURAL THEORY AND SCAFFOLDED LEARNING

The underlying theoretical foundation for this book is based on the works of Vygotsky (1978); Wood, Bruner, and Ross (1976); and sociocultural/constructivist learning theory. The basic premise of this theory is that learning takes place best within a social context where the child is paired with a more knowledgeable other. Together they work to co-construct knowledge, beginning at the child's Zone of Proximal Development or ZPD (Vygotsky, 1962) and progressively moving on to more challenging material. Within this construct the child is seen as an active participant in the learning process. The teacher's role is to gradually transfer the responsibility for learning into the child's

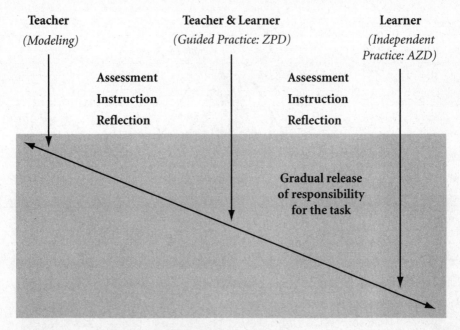

FIGURE 1.1   Model of Scaffolded Instruction
(Adapted from J. Campione, 1988. p. 104).

hands, while providing support through active modeling, guided practice, and subsequently, independent practice. Figure 1.1 depicts the processes involved in scaffolded instruction that allow the teacher to modify the child's instruction based on his or her needs at any given moment in time. It is not a linear process; rather, it is flexible and moves forward and backward depending on the child's level of understanding.

Adding to the sociocultural theorists' belief that knowledge is socially constructed, activity theory examines knowledge acquisition by breaking the process into the actual interactions or activities transpiring within a specific learning culture (Leont'ev, 1978). Therefore, the activities and the context in which they take place become vital to the learning process. While this is true for all learners, it becomes especially important for those students acquiring a second language because it ensures that they are always engaged in lessons at the appropriate instructional level within a safe, low-risk environment. The teacher is continually assessing the student's level of understanding and modifying instruction as needed. Within this model, the assessments used may be formal or informal depending on the situation. Either way, the teacher's ability to assess students on an ongoing basis is essential. Throughout this book, this type of continual assessment and evaluation will be referred to as instructional assessment.

Barbara Walker defines diagnostic teaching as "the process of using assessment and instruction at the same time to identify the instructional modifications that enable problem readers to become independent learners" (2000, p. 3). She states that diag-

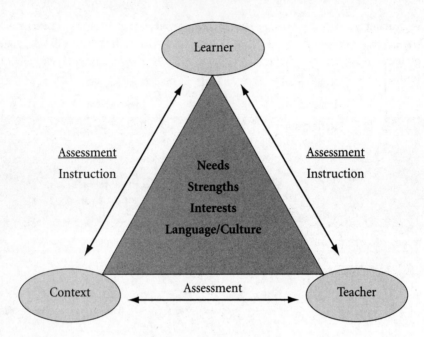

FIGURE 1.2   Instructional Assessment Model

nostic teachers are active teachers who are continually monitoring and modifying instruction as deemed necessary.

Building upon Walker's views regarding diagnostic teaching, I have expanded the definition to include the role of the learner and the sociocultural context within the learning process (see Figure 1.2). Therefore, *instructional assessment* is defined as:

> . . . a dynamic assessment and instructional process involving the interaction of the teacher and learner within a specific educational context. Instruction is focused, intensive, and active. The strengths, needs, interests, and culture of the learner heavily influence this teaching model. (Brantley, 2004)

Through this graphic it becomes apparent that the learner, the teacher, and the educational context are equally important components of the instructional assessment and teaching model. Each of the components is influenced by the learner's needs, strengths, interests, language, and culture, thus making it an individualized and dynamic model of instruction. It differs from remedial instruction in that its primary focus is not on the learner's weaknesses—where we therefore must "fix" the child to help him or her. Instead, we are working with the whole child and building upon what he or she brings to the learning situation. This distinction changes our outlook on the teaching of reading and second-language acquisition from one of a deficit model to that of a normal developmental process in which the learner progresses at his or her own pace. We see the child's needs as being a normal part of the process of reading and language acquisition rather than a problem area. This model forms the basis for the content of the remainder of the book.

REVISITING THE *CHAPTER ANTICIPATION GUIDE*

Spend a few minutes reviewing the statements presented in the Chapter Anticipation Guide at the beginning of the chapter. Compare your notes with those **highlighted.**

End-of-the-Chapter Anticipation Guide

Agree	Disagree	Statement
	✘	Approximately 10 percent of all teachers in the United States have students in their classrooms who are English Language Learners (ELLs). *Approximately 41 percent of all classroom teachers report that they have ELLs in their classrooms.*
✘		Many teachers feel unequipped to meet the needs of their ELLs. *Over 87 percent of all teachers report that they have had less than eight hours of education on the assessment and instruction of ELLs.*
	✘	Culture is an inherited set of qualities each person brings to school. *Culture is learned, on both a conscious and unconscious level, as a child grows and develops.*
✘		In order to better understand ELLs, it is important for teachers to understand their own cultures. *It is important for all educators to understand their own cultures and the ways they are impacted by culture as they teach children on a day-to-day basis.*
✘		Teachers can act as cultural mediators through the use of multicultural literature, varying participatory structures, and styles of classroom management. *Teachers who act as cultural mediators create a welcoming environment for students from all cultural and linguistic backgrounds. By creating a safe, accepting environment, teachers demonstrate to students that their cultures are valued within the classroom.*

CHAPTER TWO

Understanding the Principles of Second Language Acquisition

CHAPTER ANTICIPATION GUIDE

READ THROUGH EACH OF THE FOLLOWING STATEMENTS prior to reading the chapter. Place a checkmark in either the box labeled "agree" or "disagree" depending upon whether you believe the statement to be true or false. As you read the chapter, refer back to the chart and confirm or modify your initial responses.

Initial Chapter Anticipation Guide

Agree	Disagree	Statement
		Behaviorist learning theory of primary language acquisition is based on the premise that children learn best through stimulus, response, and reinforcement techniques.
		Language acquisition is essentially the same in the primary and secondary language.
		Second language instruction is best provided through a series of concrete and repetitive word-level tasks.
		Some theorists contend that the brain contains a "language acquisition device" that aids in the development of language skills.
		Language instruction has remained relatively unchanged over the last 100 years.

Speaking is one of the primary forms of communication for people throughout the world. Across time, oral language has been used as a means of transmitting cultural knowledge, values, and beliefs. It has allowed societies to record their histories and pass along the information to subsequent generations. As people became more mobile, languages particular to a region of the world have spread to other locations, often combining with new languages to form hybrid versions.

Language is fluid, often changing to meet the cultural and technological shifts experienced within a society at a given time in history. According to most estimates, 3,000 to 5,000 new words are added to the English language each year. Additionally, many words take on new meanings depending on the context in which they are being used and the tone, volume, and accompanying gestures of the speaker.

It is through the use of language that parents begin to acclimate their children into the family's culture and teach them skills needed for literacy development. Parents informally shape their children's language development through conversations, songs, oral stories, television, and books. In this way, children naturally start to speak—first in sounds, then words and word parts, and finally in sentences. Because most people do learn to speak at an early age through a process similar to the one just described, why is it that second language acquisition can be quite difficult? Is it the approach taken when teaching a second language or is it related to the age and context in which the second

ORAL LANGUAGE *VIGNETTE*

Stephen first began taking Spanish courses in high school. Before entering college, he had already logged in two years of Spanish instruction needed to enter the college of his choice. During his freshman and sophomore years in college, he continued his study of Spanish. By this time, he had fulfilled his language requirements for a bachelor's degree. You would think that Stephen had become a fluent speaker of Spanish at this point. Not so! While Stephen had four years of instruction under his belt, he was at best, a weak communicator in Spanish. All along Stephen had wanted to become a bilingual teacher, and now he felt cheated by his educational experiences. He set up an appointment to meet with a faculty member in the TESOL (Teaching English to Speakers of Other Languages) Department to find out what had gone wrong. Through the conversation with his advisor, Stephen came to realize that the courses he took within the program had all focused on the grammatical components of Spanish with little time spent on activities that engaged him in the use of the language. Stephen became quite proficient at conjugating verbs, but rarely spoke the language. He began to see the gaps in his knowledge base and also saw how to remedy the situation. Stephen spent the next two summers studying at a university in Mexico as part of his university's cultural exchange program. He lived in the home of a local family during his stay and became immersed in the culture and language of Mexico. At last, Stephen had achieved his goal of attaining fluency in Spanish.

language is being learned? In the following vignette, you will read about a student who has spent years trying to learn to speak Spanish and the difficulties he has encountered along the way.

Stephen's story is representative of many students' experiences when trying to learn a second language. Often language study is approached in what has been called the "grammar-based orientation" based on the following four underlying principles:

1. Learning a language means learning the grammar and the vocabulary.
2. Learning a language expands one's intellect.
3. Learning a foreign language enables one to translate great works of literature.
4. Learning the grammar of a foreign language helps one learn the grammar of one's native language. (Diller, 1978, p. 10)

In this way, students can study the vocabulary and the grammatical and syntactic structure of a language as a means of expanding their intellectual capacity (Freeman & Freeman, 1998), rather than as a means of acquiring and using the new language. This presents a very interesting dilemma for those students interested in learning to speak a

English Language Learners benefit from an academic environment that promotes the development of conversational, academic, and workplace English.

second language. For the ELLs in our classrooms, the purpose for learning to speak, read, and write in English is to be able to participate in U.S. society at all levels. This means not only acquiring conversational English, but also academic and workplace English. Without access to these varying forms of English, our ELLs will be at an economic and educational disadvantage when compared to their native English-speaking peers. Sonia Nieto (1992, 2004) states that an equal education requires more than providing "the same resources and opportunities for all students" (p. 2), but it must go further to also ensure that all students are treated fairly within the school system so that they have "the real possibility of equality of outcomes" (p. 2). It is her belief that equality of outcomes can only come to fruition within an educational system that promotes multicultural education so that all students can achieve excellence while it provides them the opportunity to "become critical and productive members of a democratic society" (Nieto, 2004, p. 2). In order for this to become a reality within schools, ELLs need to achieve *communicative competence* (Bruner, 1975; Canale, 1981; Canale & Swain, 1980) when reading, writing, listening to, and speaking in English at the following four levels: (1) grammatical competence, (2) sociolinguistic competence, (3) discourse competence, and (4) strategic competence.

Grammatical competence refers to the ability to master the *language code* (Cummins, 1981). Cummins (1981) describes the language code as "lexical items and rules of word formation, sentence formation, literal meaning, pronunciation, and spelling" (p. 7). In essence, these are the structural components of the language.

Sociolinguistic competence is related to the ability to appropriately use and understand language within a variety of contexts. The competent speaker knows the appropriate vocabulary and speech style to use in a specific situation, while the competent listener understands the meaning of varying forms of spoken and written language depending on the circumstances of its use. For example, an adult may use a more formalized pattern of speech when speaking to adults at work versus a more relaxed and off-the-cuff style of speech when talking to friends at home or in a restaurant. Proficiency in this area is shown by the ability to switch between linguistic patterns based on immediate circumstances.

Building upon sociolinguistic competence is **discourse competence.** Here the speaker and/or writer is able to organize his or her speech patterns to fit the purpose of the interaction. The same goes for the listener and the reader. They are able to derive meanings specific to the context and mode of the interaction. An example of this occurs when a student is asked to write in a specific genre using the rules of that genre. When writing an essay, it is generally necessary to begin with a topic sentence followed up with three or four supporting sentences. This pattern does not hold true for more poetic forms of writing, though. Therefore, the com-

GRAMMATICAL COMPETENCE:
The ability to understand the rules and structural components of a particular language. To develop grammatical competence, a learner must master the language at word, sentence, and literal meaning levels (Cummins, 1981).

SOCIOLINGUISTIC COMPETENCE:
Developed by learners when they are able to appropriately use the language across a variety of contexts (Cummins, 1981).

DISCOURSE COMPETENCE:
A type of linguistic competence that builds upon sociolinguistic competence through the development of an ability to read, write, speak, and understand varying language forms across differing situational circumstances (Cummins, 1978, 1981).

petent writer, reader, listener, and speaker can quickly adjust to the mode of text that is currently being presented in a given situation. Cummins (1978, 1981) was the first to distinguish between two different forms of language skills or proficiencies that need to be mastered to be truly language competent: (a) Basic Interpersonal Communicative Skills or BICS, and (b) Cognitive/Academic Language Proficiency or CALPS. *BICS* is a term used to differentiate everyday, personal communications from the more school-based, academic *CALPS* form of communication. To be truly literate in a language, a person must have mastered both forms of the language.

STRATEGIC COMPETENCE:
A language learner's ability to use a variety of linguistic strategies in order to clarify the meaning of a given communication (Cummins, 1981).

The fourth and final area of communicative competence is **strategic competence.** To have achieved strategic competence one must be able to use different strategies (paraphrasing, asking questions, repeating words or phrases) to clarify meaning when miscommunication occurs. These strategies are used naturally and serve to "compensate for breakdowns in communication" (Cummins, 1981, p. 7). Together, all four components lead to communicative competence for both primary and second language learners. So this leads to the question: How is a first language, and subsequently a second language, acquired?

The remainder of the chapter will answer this question by examining the various theories related to primary and secondary language acquisition prior to exploring the programs presently in place in schools to help ELLs become proficient in the English language.

Second-language acquisition is enhanced when an ELL is more competent in his or her primary language.

Theories of Primary Language Acquisition

The processes involved in language acquisition have been studied quite extensively in the research literature. While many of us are able to recall language lessons that occurred throughout our educational careers, we were too young to recollect the important language lessons learned from birth through kindergarten. These lessons were informal and took place within the normal context of our interactions with our environment. Because of this, many of us tend to believe that language is a learned process taught through the use of formal academic lessons, rather than a natural acquisition process that evolved over time. Various theories have been put forth in regard to language learning or acquisition beginning with behaviorist learning theories.

BEHAVIORIST APPROACH

Behaviorist learning theories are based on the works of well-known psychologist B.F. Skinner. Best known for his work with stimulus-response theories, Skinner (1957) postulated that language learning took place as a result of being exposed to a continual stream of verbal input. The learner would then imitate or mimic the language and modify it based on the feedback received from parents, siblings, and other fluent speakers in his or her immediate environment. Skinner believed that it was this repetitive stimulus–output–response cycle that allowed children to learn to speak and understand language.

TRANSFORMATIONAL GRAMMAR APPROACH (COGNITIVE APPROACH)

Since Skinner's initial writings in the 1950s, others have come along to dispute his work. Noam Chomsky (1959) refuted Skinner's theories in a seminal piece of writing by arguing that the human mind contained a specific Language Acquisition Device (LAD) that is able to unconsciously process language based on a set of grammatical rules. These rules are unconsciously learned over time as the child is exposed to fluent speakers of his or her native language. It was not until Chomsky engaged in the conversation regarding language acquisition that the cognitive approach to language development was ever addressed.

COMMUNICATIVE COMPETENCE APPROACH

In the early 1960s, Hymes (1961) built upon Chomsky's cognitive approach to language acquisition by adding a contextual component. Hymes called this the *communicative competence approach* to language acquisition. It was Hymes's contention that "the *use* of language in the social setting is important in language performance" (Díaz-Rico & Weed, 2002, p. 10). He believed that while the linguistic and grammatical components were necessary for language development, it was the use of the language within a particular social context that led to true understanding of the language. Halliday (1975) further expanded on his work by emphasizing the contextual aspect of the use of language that truly made the difference in a person's level of language competence. Together, these primary language acquisition models have added to the research base on second language acquisition (SLA). The next section details the major models of SLA, beginning with the work of Stephen Krashen.

Theories of Secondary Language Acquisition (SLA)

Much of the current research on SLA builds upon the learning theories first postulated by sociocultural researchers. For this book, I will focus on the most promising theories of second language acquisition, or SLA, that fall within the title of *communicative approaches*. First and foremost within this approach is the work of Stephen Krashen and his Monitor Model (Krashen, 1981, 1982; Krashen & Terrell, 1983). The Monitor Model consists of the following five hypotheses that provide the framework for second language acquisition:

1. The Acquisition-Learning Hypothesis
2. The Natural Order Hypothesis
3. The Monitor Hypothesis
4. The Input Hypothesis
5. The Affective Filter Hypothesis

THE ACQUISITION-LEARNING HYPOTHESIS

Within the Acquisition-Learning Hypothesis, Krashen (1981, 1982) distinguishes between the processes involved in acquiring a language versus learning a language. Acquisition is a natural process in which language is developed through real-life social interactions. Learning a language involves more structured language lessons that engage the learner is systematic, rules-based instruction.

THE NATURAL ORDER HYPOTHESIS

The Natural Order Hypothesis states that language acquisition occurs in a natural structural order based on language-specific grammatical rules. While Krashen specifies that language structures occur in "predictable sequences," these sequences are not exactly the same in first and second language acquisition (Crawford, 2005, p. 155).

THE MONITOR HYPOTHESIS

The Monitor Hypothesis serves as an internal mechanism allowing the learner to consciously monitor and modify his or her own written and oral language usage as it is being produced. Within this construct, the learner speaks or writes in the newly acquired language, and then the monitor simultaneously checks the accuracy of the language. Modifications are immediate and based on the learner's understanding of the grammatical, syntactic, and semantic features of the language.

While this theory has its detractors (Shannon, 1994; McLaughlin, 1987), many researchers support the notion of the internal language monitoring system.

THE INPUT HYPOTHESIS

COMPREHENSIBLE INPUT:
Input provided to language learners that is within their Zone of Proximal Development. This input consists of information that is generally understood by the learner (Krashen, 1982).

The Monitor Model of language acquisition contains what has been called Krashen's "most important contribution" to language theory—the Input Hypothesis (Crawford, 2005, p. 156). Within this hypothesis, Krashen makes an important distinction between the types and quality of language input a learner is exposed to during instruction and daily interactions. For language acquisition to occur, the learner must be engaged in language interactions that involve a high degree of what Krashen called *comprehensible input*. **Comprehensible input** is described as input that is clearly presented in shorter, more understandable speech patterns that are related to the learner's background knowledge. It is the combination of these elements that make the input comprehensible to the learner (Krashen, 1982).

THE AFFECTIVE FILTER HYPOTHESIS

The Affective Filter Hypothesis addresses the emotional aspects of second language acquisition. This includes such areas as a learner's motivation, level of self-confidence and efficacy toward the task of acquiring a new language, and the level of anxiety or comfort noted during the learning process (Krashen, 1981).

More recently, James Gee (1992) expanded on Krashen's theories by incorporating an enhanced sociocultural aspect based on Vygotsky's (1962) concept of the Zone of Proximal Development. Gee suggests that language acquisition is:

> . . . a process of acquiring something subconsciously by exposure to models, a process of trial and error, and practice within social groups, without formal teaching. It happens in natural settings that are meaningful and functional in the sense that acquirers know that they need to acquire the thing they are exposed to in order to function and that they in fact want to so function. (Gee, 1992, p. 113)

The process of trial and error within a supportive environment increases the likelihood a learner will successfully acquire a second language. Additionally, the more competent a learner is in his or her primary language, the more easily the second language will be acquired (Cummins, 1981).

Now, how does all of this theoretical information impact how English Language Learners (ELLs) are taught English within the school system? First, the federal government requires that all ELLs are assessed when they enter school, either at the elementary, middle, or secondary school level. While such assessments are mandated, individual states are free to select the actual test they choose to use. A variety of assessments are available to determine an ELL's level of English language development (ELD). Table 2.1 lists some of the main assessments used nationwide to calculate an ELD level.

TABLE 2.1 English Language Development Assessments

Test Name	Background Information	Purpose
IDEA	Grades Pre-K–12; NCLB compliant; standardized, norm-referenced test; individual or whole group administration.	The *IDEA* assesses English proficiency in the areas of reading, writing, listening, and speaking. It is also available in a Spanish language version.
Language Assessment Scales (LAS)	Grades K–12; NCLB compliant, individual, small group, or whole group administration.	The *LAS* measures reading, writing, listening, speaking, and English comprehension.
Woodcock-Munoz Language Survey (WMLS)	Ages 4–adult; norm-referenced, standardized test; computerized versions available.	This test is designed to measure an ELL's level of English proficiency in the areas of reading, writing, listening, and speaking. It also covers content-area knowledge/vocabulary.
California English Language Development Test (CELDT)	Individual standardized test—required for NCLB compliance.	The *CELDT* is administered to all ELLs in California on an annual basis. It tests oral and written language abilities in English.
MAC-II Test of English Language Proficiency	Ages 4–adult; norm-referenced, standardized test.	The *MAC-II* is used to test an ELL's level of English proficiency in the areas of reading, writing, listening, and speaking. It can be administered as four different subtests or all together. It also contains a quick 10-minute ELD screening test for student placement.
Secondary Level English Proficiency Test (SLEP)	Created for students at the middle, high school, and college levels. The test can be given individually or whole group.	The *SLEP* is a two-part test that was developed to measure an ELL's reading comprehension and listening comprehension levels. The test can be administered in one or two parts. Together the test takes approximately 85 minutes to administer.

(Continued)

TABLE 2.1 *(Continued)*

Test Name	Background Information	Purpose
Home Language Survey	Simple self-report form given to K–12 parents when registering their children for school. It asks parents to report the language(s) spoken at home.	The purpose of this self-report assessment is to have parents notify the school of the language(s) spoken at home in order to make initial classroom placements and determine if further testing/assessment is needed for the child.

Based on their level of English language development, ELLs need to be placed in the most appropriate school-level program or classroom situation available in a given school, school district, or state. While all states use different methods of assessing and placing students, most schools do have one of the following placements available for ELLs:

1. ESL or English as a Second Language classes or pull-out programs
2. English immersion classrooms with ELD support through modified lessons and teaching strategies
3. Bilingual classrooms taught both in English and Spanish (or another language combined with English)
4. Native language instruction with the eventual infusion of English as the learner becomes proficient in his or her native language
5. Sheltered Instruction (SI) using the Sheltered Instruction Observation Protocol (SIOP)
6. Specially Designed Academic Instruction in English (SDAIE).

The type of program used should match the level of primary and secondary language competence in the student's Basic Interpersonal Communication Skills (BICS) and Cognitive/Academic Language Proficiency (CALPS) levels. The more proficient a student is in English, the more sheltered instruction should be provided. Sheltered instruction is what provides the "bridge to the mainstream" and allows students to be "transitioned out of these programs" (Echevarria & Short, 2002, p. 6).

Regardless of the program, it is essential to provide students with a meaningful assessment and instructional program. The remainder of the book will focus on each of the areas of the language arts and how best to meet the needs of all English language learners.

REVISITING THE *CHAPTER ANTICIPATION GUIDE*

SPEND A FEW MINUTES reviewing the statements presented in the Chapter Anticipation Guide at the beginning of the chapter. Compare your notes with those **highlighted.**

End-of-the-Chapter Anticipation Guide

Agree	Disagree	Statement
✗		Behaviorist learning theory of primary language acquisition is based on the premise that children learn best through stimulus, response, and reinforcement techniques. *True—Behaviorist learning theories are based on the premise that all learning is a result of exposure to a stimulus (a speaker), responding to the stimulus (imitating the speaker or responding to the speaker), and then being positively or negatively reinforced (rewarded or corrected) for the response.*
	✗	Language acquisition is essentially the same in the primary and secondary language. *Hmmm. . . This is a tough call! Overall, many theorists believe that the processes involved in acquiring a second language are very similar to acquiring a first language. One of the main differences is in the order in which different languages are structured, and therefore acquired. I'd say this is still up for debate.*
	✗	Second language instruction is best provided through a series of concrete and repetitive word level tasks. *False—The most current language acquisition theories are based on the meaningful use of language within a series of different contexts.*
✗		Some theorists contend that the brain contains a "language acquisition device" that aids in the development of language skills. *True—Chomsky (1959) first proposed the cognitive component of language acquisition when he presented his research on the existence of a LAD or Language Acquisition Device in the human brain that aids language development.*
	✗	Language instruction has remained relatively unchanged over the last 100 years. *False—Language instruction began to evolve in the late 1950s with the development of sociolinguistic and cognitive models of language development. Instruction is much more learner-based and includes a variety of meaningful, hands-on learning activities.*

CHAPTER THREE

Instructional and Theoretical Foundations of Assessment

READ THROUGH EACH OF THE FOLLOWING STATEMENTS prior to reading the chapter. Place a checkmark in either the box labeled "agree" or "disagree" depending upon whether you believe the statement to be true or false. As you read the chapter, refer back to the chart and confirm or modify your initial responses.

Initial Chapter Anticipation Guide

Agree	Disagree	Statement
		Students and teachers face increased pressure to perform as a consequence of the implementation of standardized testing procedures.
		English Language Learners are not exempt from participation in the annual high-stakes tests.
		The terms *assessment, evaluation,* and *testing* can be used interchangeably.
		Many forms of assessment contain linguistic and cultural biases.
		Assessment and evaluation are essential components of meaningful, scaffolded instruction.

The Culture of Testing

Since the enactment of the Elementary and Secondary Education Act in 1965, U.S. schools have faced enhanced pressure to demonstrate student progress using more standardized, quantitative testing methods. Larger demands have been placed on children to perform at increasingly higher levels of achievement in reading and math, often beginning as early as kindergarten. Teachers and institutions of higher education have also felt the surge of outside pressure to "perform" wash over them.

By the 1970s, many areas of the curriculum had been distilled down to a series of discrete skills and competency standards. These skills were both hierarchical and sequential, thus making them easy to define and even easier to test for mastery (Allington, 1995). In the past thirty-five years, assessment has become a mainstay of the K–12 classroom. Students are assessed using both formal and informal assessments on a weekly, and sometimes daily, basis. While in years past teachers often created their own assessments based on the content being taught in their classrooms, schools have more recently entered the era of standardized achievement testing. Tests are rarely teacher-made, but instead are standardized and mandated at the national, state, district, and school levels. Testing is no longer just a teacher and student issue—rather, testing has become a political obsession.

It is difficult to open a newspaper or watch the evening news without the topic of academic achievement, test scores, and teacher accountability being bandied about. Both local and national politicians have made educational accountability a campaign issue as evidenced by the signing of the *No Child Left Behind Act* (NCLB) by President George W. Bush in 2001. This historic law set a new precedent by enacting the first-ever testing mandate for all students in grades 3–8 attending school in the United States. NCLB requires schools to adopt a standardized achievement test that covers both reading and mathematics and is administered on a yearly basis. Test scores must be made public by individual schools and school districts. The scores must then be disaggregated based on gender, socioeconomic status, English proficiency status, migrant status, racial and ethnic group membership, and for students with disabilities identified within the schools' student populations. While the states have the freedom to develop their own benchmarks or standards in reading and mathematics and to select or develop their own standardized assessment system, the results of the tests must reflect whether the students, and in turn the schools, are making *Adequate Yearly Progress* (AYP). Those schools that do not achieve the standards set forth by the state risk being labeled as "failing schools," which may impact their ability to receive federal educational funding (Stiggins, 2005).

The present political-educational climate has created what I describe as the **culture of testing**. This construct refers to an increased focus on standardized testing and test scores; the arbitrary creation of multilayered grade level standards across the curriculum; and a decreased emphasis on

CULTURE OF TESTING:
A high-pressure educational environment created by an increased emphasis on student and teacher accountability. The present culture of testing has placed an increased amount of emphasis on the development of state standards, high-stakes testing, and the use of rigid curricular programs (Brantley, 2004).

meaningful, authentic, and student-centered learning. The advent of the culture of testing set into motion by the NCLB Act has impacted schools, teachers, and students in several *less than ideal* ways. Popham (2001) describes these unintended outcomes as follows:

1. Misdirected pressures on educators
2. Misidentification of inferior and superior schools
3. Curricular reductionism
4. Drill-and-kill instructional techniques
5. Test-pressured cheating (pp. 16-23)

While Popham is not against the use of standardized testing as one method of gathering information on a student's progress, he believes that the results are often misused and misrepresented by those outside the classroom. This has led to many negative and unfair educational consequences for teachers and students, especially those students for whom English is a second language.

So . . . within the present culture of testing, how can teachers create a bias-free classroom assessment system that promotes meaningful instruction for English Language Learners? I believe the answer lies in the research on teaching and learning. For decades, educators and psychologists have been studying the cognitive development of children, beginning at birth and extending into adulthood. Emerging from this body of literature is research on the collaborative nature of instruction and assessment. When we understand this relationship, it becomes clear how and why we should and should not assess learners. To begin with, let's focus on the hows and whys of assessment and then differentiate between authentic or educative assessment, evaluation, and testing.

Differentiating among Assessment, Evaluation, and Testing

Wiggins (1998) begins to address the aims, or whys, of assessment when he describes *educative assessment* as follows:

> An **educative assessment system** is designed to teach—to improve performance (of student and teacher) and evoke exemplary pedagogy. It is built on the bedrock of meaningful performance tasks that are credible and realistic (authentic), hence engaging to students. (p.12)

It should be noted that an educative assessment system includes both the teacher and the learner as active participants in the assessment process, thereby making it a collaborative effort that is used to support meaningful teaching and learning within the classroom. Additionally, Wiggins distinguishes educative assessment as a "system"

An educative assessment system incorporates the processes of assessment and evaluation into the activities students participate in on a daily basis.

rather than a series of disconnected tests and assignments that lie outside the realm of instruction. By incorporating such a system of assessment into the curriculum, the act of assessing a student becomes integral to the act of teaching a student. Together teaching, learning, and assessing are commingled throughout the instructional day, allowing both teachers and students to continually monitor and reflect upon their understandings. It is this process of collaborative–reflective learning that serves as the basis for scaffolded instruction (Wood, Bruner, & Ross, 1976). Within a meaningful classroom assessment system, the process of continually **evaluating** the assessment results in a timely manner is imperative.

EVALUATION:
The process of systematically analyzing assessment results in order to provide relevant instruction. Evaluation requires one to consider strengths and needs.

When evaluating assessment results, the teacher makes note of the student's strengths and areas of need. While this may seem to be common sense, assessments have often been used to identify weaknesses with little regard for the strengths demonstrated by the results. By building on a student's areas of strength, a teacher can augment the student's foundational skills while introducing new materials, skills, and concepts. For example, by building on the student's first language skills in reading, such as the ability to decode phonetic words in the primary language, the teacher can introduce new phonetic words in English. This allows the learner to be successful while learning the new language and validates his or her native language abilities. It is a win–win situation for both the teacher and the learner. With success comes an increased level of efficacy and motivation for the student, which tends to lead to a willingness to try new things.

In an attempt to clarify the terms assessment, evaluation, and testing, it is valuable to look at the processes and outcomes involved in each construct. **Assessment** is an ongoing process of both formal and informal performance measures that are evaluated in order to provide appropriate classroom instruction.

Testing, on the other hand, is a type of assessment that has been "used for nearly a century to quickly and efficiently measure knowledge and simple applications of skills" (Taylor & Nolen, 2005, p. 152). Tests are used as a measure of the amount of knowledge gleaned from a particular concept, unit, or skill taught by a teacher. They often serve as the culminating experience for students. Tests can also be more diagnostic in nature. In this case, they are used to identify a student's needs in a particular area of the curriculum such as reading, spelling, or math. Additionally, tests are used to calculate a student's grades for reporting purposes. Tests are valuable if and when the results are used to improve instruction and student achievement.

Evaluation is the systematic processes of filtering out the relevant data collected through testing and assessment and analyzing it for the purpose of providing students with meaningful and appropriate instruction. It is through this final step of evaluation that the information gathered from various forms of assessment and testing becomes valuable to the teacher and the learner. Without this final step, the data collected is useless.

Instructional Assessment Tools

Assessment is a necessary and valuable part of classroom instruction. With that being said, it can also have very negative consequences on our students if there is a "mismatch between assessment tools and instruction" (Taylor & Nolen, 2005, p. 8). Taylor and Nolen describe the negative consequences of this mismatch as leaving some students at a loss for making sense of what is being taught in school because they cannot see a link between school and the real world. This occurs when students are assessed using methods that are completely unrelated to their lives, leaving them feeling devalued and unattached to the school experience. This mismatch can also occur when students are asked to turn in essays or written responses to literature as a means of demonstrating the written language abilities or their understanding of a piece of literature in their daily class work, but are then asked to complete a multiple choice test as a way of grading them on these same skills. To prevent the negative consequences of assessment, teachers need to be very thoughtful when creating a classroom assessment system. This requires an in-depth understanding of the four main characteristics of assessments and the types of assessment structures available to teachers. We'll begin our discussion by taking a look at the four main characteristics of assessment that have the greatest impact on a student's ability to demonstrate what they have learned. Next we'll look at the two main structural categories of assessment: formal and informal (or alternative). This section will end by detailing the four main assessment domains.

Characteristics of Assessments

Gredler and Johnson (2004) describe the four main characteristics of assessments that must be considered when creating a meaningful and appropriate classroom assessment system. While this is not specific to ELLs, it is essential for all learners in order to provide students with a fair and valuable system of assessment.

POSSIBLE RESPONSE FORMATS
- *Interviews*
- *Fill-in-the-blank*
- *Prompt writing*
- *Demonstrations*
- *Open-ended questions*
- *Visual representations*

To begin with, teachers need to consider the *response format* when selecting an appropriate assessment. The response format may vary depending upon the task being measured and the particular student population being assessed (Gredler & Johnson, 2004, p. 20). For example, if a sixth-grade student has recently emigrated to the United States from Mexico and speaks only Spanish, it would seem prudent to assess the student's level of reading comprehension in his or her native language. Asking the student to read a passage in English and write a written response in English would likely produce little or no response on the part of the student. It would also needlessly upset the student and would not present the teacher with any useful instructional information. Additionally, a problem can occur when students are assessed using formats that they are unfamiliar with because these formats do not exist in the schools in their home countries. For example, in many Middle Eastern countries the multiple choice exam does not exist, therefore making this an unfair form of assessment for these students.

Because of these issues, the response format should match the needs and abilities of the student as well as the skill, concept, or task being measured. Considering the response format will increase the likelihood of success for both the teacher and the student by decreasing the level of stress associated with the assessment.

The second characteristic to consider is the *situational circumstances* in which the assessment will take place. This characteristic refers to the environmental context (whole group, small group, one-on-one) of the assessment. Many students are more comfortable working in a small group, while others prefer to work one-on-one with the teacher. Therefore, the context is best matched to the needs of the student. This ties in nicely with the third characteristic, the *time requirements* of the assessment. It is essential to provide students with ample time to complete the task so as not to compromise the results (Gredler & Nolen, 2004, p. 20). Again, some cultures do not place time limits on students taking an exam; thus, timing an exam can add an additional level of complexity to a task.

The final characteristic to consider when selecting an assessment is the *clarity of the directions.* Students can perform poorly on a task purely because the directions are vague, confusing, or overwhelming (Gredler & Nolen, 2004, p. 20). It would be beneficial to read the directions prior to administering an assessment to determine their level of clarity. It may be necessary to modify the directions if they will cause confusion as to the true nature of the task. The clearer the directions, the more likely the students will perform successfully. This may mean that the directions will need to be read in a student's native language. Often directions contain content area vocabulary that may prove to be indecipherable to the ELL, causing that student to shut down or misconstrue the task. This is a simple way of decreasing the complexity of the task, although not all forms of assessment will allow for such modifications. In fact, many formal assessments have standardized directions to ensure the reliability of their results. You'll want to refer to the individual instruction manuals to determine whether you have the flexibility to modify the instructions. In the following section you will find a description of the different types of assessments so you can decide which are the most appropriate for your students.

Formal Assessments

VALIDITY:
The extent to which a test or other assessment measures what it is intended to measure. Ask yourself: Does this really measure the skill, concept, or level of understanding that it is supposed to measure? (Gunning, 2002; Thorndike, 2005)

RELIABILITY:
The level of consistency in the results of a particular measure. Ask yourself: Does this measure consistently yield similar results when used with the same student or same group of students? (Gunning, 2002; Thorndike, 2005)

Formal assessments are those assessments that are designed to be given to students in a very structured format. They are preplanned, and their purpose and administration procedures are well known to the teacher and the students (Mertler, 2003). Oosterhof (1999) believes that it is the level of premeditation that distinguishes a formal assessment from an informal assessment. Formal assessments have often been referred to as "traditional assessments" (Mertler, 2003, p. 10). Within the category of formal assessments are three, sometimes overlapping subcategories: standardized tests, norm-referenced tests, and criterion-referenced tests. While all norm-referenced tests are also standardized tests, only some criterion-referenced tests are also standardized tests. The next section will establish the commonalities and differences in the different types of tests.

STANDARDIZED TESTS

Standardized tests are "designed to be given according to a standard set of circumstances. These tests have sets of directions, which are to be followed exactly. They may also have time limits"(Gunning, 2002, p. 75). Generally, standardized tests have been researched and tested out on various student populations in order to make modifications as needed. The end result is that you are left with tests that have a high degree of **validity** an **reliability**.

NORM-REFERENCED TESTS

All norm-referenced tests are also standardized tests. Norm-referenced tests serve what Gunning (2002) refers to as a "sorting function" (p. 74). This means that these tests are used to group students according to their various levels of achievement. Often schools and school districts use norm-referenced tests as a means of comparing their student achievement levels to those of students in comparable school districts. Popham (2001) notes that there are several weaknesses to using norm-referenced tests to gauge the success of schools and their educational programs. First, norm-referenced tests are comprised of test items that only 40 to 60 percent of the norm group accurately answered. This means that the test items that most students were able to answer correctly were removed from the test. Second, these tests are designed to create a bell-curve response pattern, thus ensuring that most students will score in the average or 50 percent range. Third, because all students at a particular grade level are tested on the same material, it's possible that many students are being tested on material not covered in their school's curriculum, leading to misinformation on their abilities. Keeping these factors in mind, teachers and administrators must be aware of the true nature of norm-referenced tests when interpreting the results.

CRITERION-REFERENCED TESTS

Criterion-referenced tests are constructed to measure a student's performance against a preestablished standard or criterion. They differ from norm-referenced tests in that they do not compare students with one another. In a criterion-referenced test, the score needed to meet, exceed, or not pass the standard is discretionary and therefore subjective (Gunning, 2002). For example, while one teacher may require kindergarten students to name 80 percent of the letters of the alphabet by the winter break, another teacher may not require that level of accuracy until the spring break. They are both teaching the same skills but each has set a different criterion for judging the student's abilities at a given point in time. The flexibility offered with a criterion-referenced test offers teachers more opportunity to use the results to guide classroom instruction.

Some tests, such as Marie Clay's *Observation Survey* (2002), are both a standardized test and a criterion-referenced test. This is because of the specificity of the directions and the fact that it is normed against a representative group of first-grade students, while also setting up specific criteria for the number of items students should be able to complete at a specific age level. In this case, the task is the same for all of the test-takers, but the judgment criteria change depending on the child's age.

Alternative Assessments

In the last section we discussed the more formal or traditional forms of assessment. Now we will move our focus into the arena of alternative assessments. **Alternative**

**ALTERNATIVE
ASSESSMENTS:**
*A category of assessments
that are more informal in
nature and often take
place within the normal
process of instructing
students. Alternative
assessments include but
are not limited to check-
lists, observations, teacher-
made assessments,
performances, student and
peer assessments, and
demonstrations. These are
nonstandardized forms of
assessment that provide
data in a timely manner.*

assessments are the newer forms of assessment that came into favor in the 1960s and 1970s when schools began to explore more experiential, student-centered learning experiences. The traditional paper-and-pencil assessments no longer matched the newer teaching techniques, so teachers looked for more realistic, or authentic, means of assessing students (Mertler, 2003). This led to the development of more informal assessment processes.

INFORMAL ASSESSMENTS

Informal assessments provide the teacher with a high degree of flexibility in the administration and scoring procedures. Generally, time limits are not introduced, and directions may be modified to meet the needs of the particular group of students being assessed. These assessments tend to require more time to score and evaluate because of the more informal and authentic nature of the tasks. Informal assessments generally include observational assessments, performance assessments, self-assessment, and portfolios.

OBSERVATIONAL ASSESSMENTS

Observational assessments are used to document a student's academic and affective behaviors both in the classroom and during activities outside of the classroom. The observations may involve the use of "checklists, rating scales, and observational notes" (Taylor & Nolen, 2005, p. 132). The purpose of engaging in observational assessments is to capture the student's actual performance as he or she is engaged in a task. It allows the teacher to document growth and change that may not be visible on a more structured or formal assessment.

SELF-ASSESSMENT

Sociocultural learning theory (Vygotsky, 1962) embraces the notion that students are active participants in their own learning and therefore should have some decision-making power in their educational program. To promote active engagement of students, teachers must encourage them to become *self-regulated learners.* Self-regulated learners are capable of judging their performance in relation to goals they have set for themselves through self-observation and the continual reflection upon and modification of goals they have set (Borich & Tombari, 2004, pp. 17–18). Through this process students become aware of their strengths and needs and can therefore become more invested in their own education. Often, self-regulating students keep a journal of their progress along with checklists and work samples that are indicative of their past and present levels of performance. These samples are then stored in their portfolios and revisited as needed.

PORTFOLIOS AND WORK FOLDERS

Portfolios have been used in many forms for several years. Often the term has been considered synonymous with the terms "work folder" or "writing folder," but that can be a bit misleading. Portfolios are clearly defined as follows:

> . . . a purposeful collection of student work that tells the story of the student's efforts, progress, or achievement in given area[s]. This collection must include student participation in selection of portfolio content; the guidelines for selection; the criteria for judging merit; and evidence of student reflection. (Arter & Spandel, 1992, p. 36)

Within Arter's and Spandel's (1992) definition of a portfolio it is worth noting the importance of the student in the processes of selection, evaluation, and reflection. This is what differentiates a portfolio from a work folder, in which teacher-selected student samples are stored. Portfolios will be discussed in more depth in Chapter 10 as we put them to use as a means of assessing ELLs' progress in writing.

Assessment Domains

Now that we have looked at the various types of assessment, it is time to delve deeper into domains of assessment: achievement tests, aptitude tests, affective assessments, and performance assessments. You may find that some of the domains overlap with the structures of assessment presented in the previous section. I believe this shows the complexities involved in accurately assessing students in order to develop a picture of the whole student. This discussion will begin by taking a look at achievement tests.

ACHIEVEMENT TESTS

Achievement tests are designed to measure "what a person has learned to do" (Thorndike, 2005, p. 60). Achievement tests are specific to a particular skill, content area, or curriculum program, and the results may change across time. This type of test is given to students for a specific reason—to measure their level of mastery in one or more areas of the curriculum. Ideally, after receiving further instruction, a student's scores should improve.

Achievement tests can serve two distinct purposes for teachers: formative evaluation and summative evaluation. *Formative evaluations* are administered throughout the instructional process to measure the student's learning at different points in time. Teachers then use the results to guide instruction by noting the student's strengths and areas of need and modifying the instruction as needed.

Summative evaluations are generally the culminating assessments given at the end of a unit of study. They seek to measure overall learning and are often used to grade a student. For example, after studying a unit on the Revolutionary War in fifth grade, a teacher may prepare an exam to test the amount of material learned about the war. The test may contain a matching section in which the students are presented with a list of content area vocabulary that they are supposed to match with the correct definition. Next, they may have a multiple choice section containing fact-based questions about specific people, places, and events of note. The exam may conclude with a short essay section where students are asked to discuss how a particular person (John Hancock, George Washington) or event (the Boston Tea Party) impacted the colonists and their decision to enter into a war with the British. Many teachers use a combination of both summative and formative evaluations, depending upon the intended outcomes they are seeking (Thorndike, 2005).

APTITUDE TESTS

Aptitude tests are considered to provide *predictive evidence* of a student's potential to perform a distinct task or skill in the future (Mertler, 2003, p. 54). Because of the predictive nature, purpose, and content of an aptitude test, it is considered to be a criterion-referenced test. This type of test is often used to place students in classes for the gifted and talented or special education (IQ—Intelligence Quotient tests), as a gatekeeper for entrance to college (SAT—Scholastic Aptitude Test), or to determine a person's aptitude for a particular job (GATB—General Aptitude Battery Test). In effect, the results are used to infer a person's ability to do something that he or she has yet to attempt.

AFFECTIVE ASSESSMENTS

Affective assessments are those assessments that address the student's dispositions, motivation, values, beliefs, and self-concept in relation to learning. Often because of the personal nature of this domain, a teacher must rely on self-reports by students and observations of their behaviors both inside and outside of the classroom. Even though the affective components of learning may be difficult to assess and evaluate, they are often very essential components of the learning process. Much research has been done in the area of motivation and learning. Overwhelmingly, research supports the notion that when a student feels engaged in relevant learning experiences and feels competent to successfully complete the activities, that student becomes more intrinsically motivated to perform. Generally, increased motivation ultimately leads to increased performance (Deci & Ryan, 1985, 1987; Ryan, Koestner, & Nolen, 2003; Deci, 1991).

PERFORMANCE ASSESSMENTS

Performance assessments are those assessments that closely relate to real-life experiences. "The difference between a performance and a performance assessment is whether the performance goes beyond a set of directions (expectations) to guide all students' work and includes a set of rules for scoring (evaluating) the performance" (Taylor & Nolen, 2005, p. 83). By adding the explicit assessment piece to a performance, students see the performance as a fun activity, and also as a valued means of transmitting their level of knowledge in a specific area. Taylor and Nolen (2005) suggest setting performance expectations with the students prior to engaging in the activity so students are aware of the goals and expectations up front. This might include developing a set of performance directions a rubric denoting the levels of performance expectations (does not meet expectations, meets expectations, and/or exceeds expectations) or delineating the steps involved in successfully performing the activity.

Examples of performances to which these assessment guidelines refer include, but are not limited to, the following:

1. Plays and musical performances
2. Creation of written or artistic artifacts
3. Participation in a simulation experience or real-life situation such as would be involved in service learning
4. Cooking, sewing, playing football, and other activity-based experiences

By adding specific performance-based criteria, the students are more likely to achieve a higher level of success.

To summarize assessment, evaluation, and testing, it is important to keep in mind that the purpose for implementing a classroom assessment system is to improve instruction and student achievement. If a measure does not serve that purpose, it has no place in the classroom.

Culture-Fair Assessment Practices

A question that often arises when discussing the assessment of linguistically and culturally diverse populations pertains to the "fairness" of a particular assessment tool. Test items may refer to stories, rhymes, historical events, music, pictures, objects, and language-specific terminology that are known only to those from the mainstream culture. Students coming from varying linguistic, socioeconomic, and cultural backgrounds may not have been exposed to these cultural artifacts and therefore may be at a disadvantage when taking certain tests. These biases may be overt or may be quite subtle; regardless, they can negatively impact the performance of students from diverse backgrounds (Díaz-Rico & Weed, 2002). It is up to the educational community, and more often than not the classroom teacher, to provide ELLs with culturally fair assessments. Many times these biases can be addressed by incorporating a balance of formal and informal assessments into the classroom curriculum. In the end, teachers do want to be able to accurately assess and evaluate the strengths and needs of the ELLs within their classrooms so as to provide them with meaningful, relevant, and developmentally appropriate instruction.

REVISITING THE *CHAPTER ANTICIPATION GUIDE*

SPEND A FEW MINUTES reviewing the statements presented in the chapter antici-pation guide at the beginning of the chapter. Compare your notes with those **highlighted** below.

End-of-the-Chapter Anticipation Guide

Agree	Disagree	Statement
✗		Students and teachers face increased pressure to perform as a consequence of the implementation of standardized testing procedures. *True—Because of the increased demands placed on teachers and students by the No Child Left Behind Act (2001), students are being tested more frequently. With increased testing comes more of an emphasis on increasing achievement levels on tests in the areas of reading, math, and writing. If students do not score so as to meet the school's AYP goals, the school, and subsequently the students and teachers, are labeled as failing.*
✗		English language learners are not exempt from participation in the annual high-stakes tests. *True—Overall, ELLs are not exempt from participation in the standardized tests mandated through the federal government. Test scores are disaggregated by the students' grade level, socioeconomic status, gender, ethnicity, and language status. It is therefore required to test ELLs and report their test scores.*
	✗	The terms *assessment, evaluation,* and *testing* can be used interchangeably. *False—Assessment refers to the act of collecting data on a student's progress through multiple data sources. Evaluation refers to the analysis and interpretation of the data collected on a student or group of students. Testing is a specific type of assessment such as a standardized, norm-referenced, and/or criterion-referenced test.*
✗		Many forms of assessment contain linguistic and cultural biases. *True—Many tests and other forms of assessment contain inherent linguistic and cultural biases. They are often con-structed based on the norms, values, and knowledge base of the mainstream culture.*

Agree	Disagree	Statement
✗		Assessment and evaluation are essential components of meaningful, scaffolded instruction. *True—in order to provide ELLs and all other students with appropriate instruction, a meaningful assessment system must be in place. This requires the teacher to use multiple assessment measures that look at the whole child. The assessment results must then be evaluated and used to guide the classroom instruction.*

CHAPTER FOUR

Oral Language and Vocabulary Assessment and Development

Read through each of the following statements prior to reading the chapter. Place a checkmark in either the box labeled "agree" or "disagree" depending upon whether you believe the statement to be true or false. As you read the chapter, refer back to the chart and confirm or modify your initial responses.

Initial Chapter Anticipation Guide

Agree	Disagree	Statement
		Vocabulary instruction is divided into two distinct parts: receptive vocabulary and expressive vocabulary.
		ELLs go through several phases of language development. The first phase is the silent phase in which they listen and do not respond.
		Most children acquire approximately 500 new vocabulary words per year prior to entering kindergarten.
		The ability to listen to language is related to a person's ability to acquire vocabulary in his or her primary and secondary languages.

VIGNETTE

Tran was an international student who was in the United States to earn a master's degree in TESOL or Teaching English to Students of Other Languages. As a part of his course work, he was asked to work in the university's Literacy Center as a tutor for a middle school student. Uncomfortable with his own level of English proficiency, Tran was hesitant to participate in the required practicum. Just days before he was to begin tutoring, he was pleasantly surprised when his professor addressed his concerns with the whole class. Initially, he thought that the professor could read his mind or that someone had shared his concerns with her, but as she spoke, he realized that he was not alone. After working with students from around the world for many years, his professor was quite aware of many of the concerns faced by students/teachers who are not native speakers of English but want to teach in English. Over the years students had shared their concerns in journal entries, reader responses, and through classroom conversations. By implementing a few strategies into her own classroom instruction, she was able to support her international students and ensure that the middle school students would receive high-quality tutoring instruction. So how was she able to accomplish this seemingly impossible feat? Read on to find out!

Tran's professor, being a second language student herself, had picked up several academic coping strategies as she had progressed through school. First, she would read all of the assigned texts prior to attending the class lecture on the topic. By reading the material ahead of time, she had exposed herself to the vocabulary needed to understand the lecture to be given in class that day. Using this strategy, she asked her own students to do the same thing, thus providing them with time to build their background knowledge and therefore comprehend more of the class lecture. As she shared her experiences with her own students, they began to brainstorm strategies that they could use to prepare for the tutoring sessions with their middle school tutees. First, they would select a fictional text for use with their tutees over the course of the semester and hold book club meetings among themselves in order to understand the literal and inferential aspects of the text prior to reading it with their tutees. Their goal was to always be at least one chapter ahead of the tutees so they would never be caught unprepared. Next, together they would develop questions based on the text for use during their sessions with the tutees. The questions would be created using the four levels of questioning (Right There, Think & Search, Author and Me, and On My Own questions) described in the Question-Answer Response Strategy (QAR) by Raphael (1984). The questions would be written on sticky notes and placed in the appropriate stopping places in the text. Last, the students and their instructor developed conversation prompts and writing prompts for each chapter. They would engage in a conversation based on these prompts prior to asking their tutees to respond to them orally and/or in writing. Through this process of modeling, practice, and engagement, the international tutors were able to successfully tutor middle school students in English while simultaneously improving their own English language abilities. It turned out to be a win–win situation for everyone involved, although it could have turned out very differently if they had not been engaged in such a rich language learning experience themselves.

The vignette demonstrates the power of good instruction along with the need to develop both content area vocabulary and oral language skills for ELLs at all stages of language development. In the remainder of the chapter, assessments and strategies for developing these skills are addressed at length.

Functions of Language

Language is one of the primary tools for the transmission of cultural values, beliefs, and attitudes. It is also the means by which we develop our cognitive and social functions (Mead, 1977; Vygotsky, 1978). A person's capacity to use the standard form of English is often seen as a litmus test to determine his or her level of cognitive capability. Because of this type of deficit thinking, students from linguistically diverse backgrounds have often been marginalized within the school system.

Shirley Brice Heath's (1983) seminal ethnographic study, entitled *Ways with Words: Language, Life and Work in Communities and Classrooms,* made visible the educational implications of taking such a deficit approach to the education of linguistically and culturally diverse students. Heath explored the communication patterns of children from homes in which standard English was not used and where the patterns of communication differed from the mainstream population. She noted that the children from diverse backgrounds often communicated in a more circular fashion rather than the more linear communication patterns found in schools and mainstream United States. Once the children entered school, they were often seen as being less intelligent and inherently less able to engage in more complex and abstract learning situations. The end result of such deficit thinking led to an inferior quality of education being provided to students from culturally and linguistically diverse backgrounds, even within the same four classroom walls as the children from more "mainstream" backgrounds (Heath, 1983).

In an attempt to supersede such deficit thinking, accurate assessment of a student's language proficiency level becomes a powerful tool. Initially, the assessment should be geared toward determining the student's English language proficiency level, and then his or her primary language proficiency level. In this way, the teacher can look at the discrepancies between the student's English language and native language abilities. This discrepancy shows a level of potential.

Related to an ELL's oral language proficiency level is his or her level of vocabulary mastery in his or her first and second languages. Oftentimes, children with a limited vocabulary experience difficulties across all areas of the language arts, thus making this an area to focus on when assessing oral language proficiency. To begin with, it is necessary to develop an in-depth understanding of the components of vocabulary: receptive vocabulary versus expressive vocabulary. While they are interrelated, there are many components that make each type of vocabulary distinct as well.

Vocabulary Development

According to Frank Smith (1987), most children acquire a speaking and listening vocabulary of over 10,000 words by the time they reach kindergarten. He goes on to say that the numbers may vary depending upon the socioeconomic status of the children and whether they may have learning difficulties. Once children enter school, it is estimated that they learn anywhere from 1,500 to 8,000 new vocabulary words per year (Clark, 1993; Johnson, 2001; Nagy, Herman, & Anderson, 1985). Again, the variations in numbers are dependent on a variety of social and educational factors.

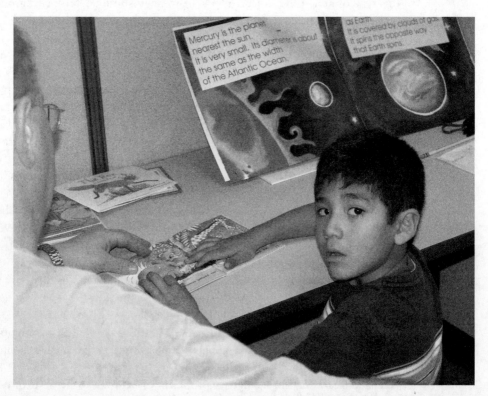

Vocabulary is enhanced through the use of rich conversations based on narrative and expository texts.

While we would like to think that all of this learning takes place as a result of rich conversations, educational lessons, and reading, some of the vocabulary is acquired in "less than educational" circumstances. By this I am referring to television programs that use a lot of slang or more common conversational language and movies with G, PG, PG-13, and R ratings. Much oral language is also learned on the playground, in the lunchroom, and when hanging out with peers in different venues. Regardless of the context, children acquire language through listening, speaking, reading, and writing. Cooter and Flynt (1996) divided the four kinds of vocabulary into two main categories based on their respective functions: receptive vocabulary and expressive vocabulary. *Receptive vocabulary* is a term used to describe a more passive type of vocabulary function in which a person can *listen* to words and/or *read* words and understand their meaning without being required to "use" the word(s) in oral or written conversation (Cooter & Flynt, 1996). According to Reutzel and Cooter (2003), listening vocabulary is the largest of all of the forms of vocabulary "housed in one's mind and usable for language transactions" (p. 226). Therefore, the listening vocabulary level provides the basis for the formation of each of the other types of vocabulary.

The second main category of vocabulary is *expressive vocabulary*. Expressive vocabulary consists of both *speaking* and *writing* vocabulary. Within this category, a person is required to produce language, either in writing or in speech. Not only must the person have the word housed in his or her listening vocabulary, he or she must then feel comfortable enough with its meaning and correct usage to incorporate it into a conversation or piece of text. This requires a higher degree of understanding. You may be able to recall a particular word that you've heard over and over again and also seen in print but have yet to use in a conversation. It may be because you are uncomfortable with the word's pronunciation or clear meaning that prevents you from using the word in a conversation. Can you think of an example of a word you were uncomfortable using as part of your oral vocabulary? I can—it was the word *hegemony.* In my doctoral program, several of my professors referred to this concept and assigned texts containing this word over a four-year period. It was not until I had one particular professor create a drawing of a man standing with his right foot in one canoe and his left foot in another canoe trying to keep his balance that it all came together for me. He was describing the fine balance needed to manage the inherent power structures involved in teaching adults (in this case) that I really understood hegemony and hegemonic relationships. Since that time I have used the word in the courses I teach as well as in my writing, but as you can see, it was a long process. While all words don't require such a depth of understanding, we all go through a similar process when acquiring new vocabulary words. Keep this process in mind as you work with ELLs in your classroom because it will also help you to understand why they remain silent for so long as they are learning English.

Before delving into the assessments available to measure receptive and expressive vocabulary levels, it would be useful to note the stages of language development ELLs progress through while acquiring English as their second language.

Stages of Language Development

Many researchers agree that second language acquisition proceeds through a series of developmental stages:

1. Preproduction
2. Early production
3. Speech emergence
4. Intermediate fluency
5. Advanced fluency (Hurley & Tinajero, 2001; Krashen & Terrell, 1983; Terrell, 1977)

While ELLs move through these same stages, they do so at varying speeds (Thomas & Collier, 1997) and in differing patterns. Tinajero and Schifini (1997) contend that many ELLs have growth "spurts and lags" as a natural part of language acquisition. It is the teacher's role to note these spurts and lags through continual assessment and provide appropriate instruction to stimulate further growth (Tinajero & Hurley, 2001, p. 33).

In order to keep abreast of the ELL's progress, a teacher would benefit from understanding the five stages of language acquisition. This knowledge would serve to guide the teacher to select relevant assessments and developmentally appropriate instructional strategies. The next section will describe each stage of development. While the stages appear linear, keep in mind the recursive nature of language acquisition as you read through them.

PREPRODUCTION

The preproduction stage is often referred to as the *silent stage* of language acquisition. An ELL within this stage may have some verbal abilities in his or her second language but generally responds through the use of gestures, pointing to pictures, objects, or people and by drawing pictures of what he or she is trying to communicate. This is a natural part of language acquisition as the learner spends much time engaged in "active listening" in order to begin to learn new vocabulary and comprehend the complexities of new surroundings (Tinajero & Hurley, 2001). Keep in mind that the length of the preproduction stage will vary depending on the learner.

Teachers can assist ELLs who are in this stage by surrounding them with a great deal of comprehensible input in the form of visual aids; high-interest materials based on the learners' background knowledge; and alternate forms of instruction that utilize music, movement, and artifacts (Crawford, 2005). Not only will this help ELLs to acquire new English vocabulary, but it will also engage them in the learning process.

EARLY PRODUCTION

As soon as ELLs begin to feel more comfortable in their new surroundings and have started to develop a solid listening vocabulary, they will begin to respond verbally. Generally, their first responses will take the form of one- or two-word statements, often in response to questions being posed in more informal settings. For example, at this stage of development, Tinajero and Hurley (2001) suggest asking simple "yes and no, either/or, or listing-type questions" related to daily activities and events (p. 34).

Krashen and Terrell (1983) caution teachers against correcting ELLs' errors at this stage of development because it may cause them to shut down, thus sending them back into the silent period of development. It is more beneficial to model the correct English vocabulary and pronunciation in much the same way parents model standard English to young children as they are learning to speak. Once the students feel comfortable speaking in single words and small phrases, they may proceed into the speech emergence stage.

SPEECH EMERGENCE

Throughout the first two stages of language development, ELLs have been acquiring an increasingly larger listening vocabulary. As they have become more comfortable with the language, they have "tried it out" in parts and pieces. In the third stage, ELLs begin to speak in more complex phrases and sentences, often engaging in conversation on a variety of topics that fall within their comfort zone.

Terrell (1981) suggests that teachers engage students in activities that rely heavily on multiple uses of language. Some of the activities suggested are games, plays, music, discussions, and other forms of language play. It would be beneficial to begin with more playful uses of language prior to moving into areas of the curriculum that require ELLs to learn and use more complex content area vocabulary. The more complex language should be addressed in the intermediate and advanced fluency levels of language acquisition.

INTERMEDIATE FLUENCY

At the fourth stage of language acquisition, ELLs have a well-developed listening vocabulary level and a fairly solid speaking vocabulary level. They have gained insights into the structure of the language and the nuances specific to English so that they are now able to converse with a high degree of comprehension and fluency. ELLs generally feel comfortable enough to read some materials and are beginning to write in English.

Tinajero and Hurley (2001) suggest that ELLs in the intermediate fluency stage begin to read, write, and speak in a narrative genre prior to delving into the arena of expository texts. Teachers can introduce new vocabulary through the use of various strategies such as read-alouds, questioning techniques, choral and echo reading, word

Read-alouds are a powerful tool for developing a student's receptive vocabulary level. They can be used for students of all age and grade levels.

games, graphic organizers, and other strategies known to enhance vocabulary development. As the students continue to develop language fluency, they will progress into the final and advanced stage of language acquisition.

ADVANCED FLUENCY

In this final stage, ELLs are considered to have fully acquired the English language. They are now prepared to read and write different textual genres because they have an in-depth understanding of the grammar, syntax, pragmatic, and semantic features of the English language. While they are quite fluent in speaking the language, this does not mean that they are "finished" learning English. This is a time to provide enrichment activities to build upon their present level of knowledge and delve into the more abstract areas of the language. It is also a time to learn complex content area information through analysis and critical literacy strategies. ELLs can now be taught to create new understandings based on a particular knowledge base and generalize these understandings to new areas. It is an exciting time in the language acquisition process for all involved.

The stage is now set for determining the appropriate assessments for ELLs as they progress through the five stages of English language acquisition. Because ELLs start in the preproduction or silent period, we will begin by looking at those assessments best suited for learners in this stage of development. This takes us to the area of receptive vocabulary assessment, or more specifically, listening vocabulary assessments.

Listening Vocabulary Assessments

Relatively few assessments are available for measuring a student's receptive (listening) vocabulary level. Most use picture clues rather than oral language during administration. One such test is the *Peabody Picture Vocabulary Test-III (PPVT-III)*, which is available in both Spanish and English (Dunn & Dunn, 1997). Both versions of the test are normed for preschool-aged children through adulthood. The *PPVT-III* is an untimed test in which a student is given a set of four pictures to look at as the examiner reads a word aloud. For example, the word read aloud may be "horse." The page would contain four pictures and the child would be asked to point to the horse (see Figure 4.1).

FIGURE 4.1 **Sample Page Adapted from the *PPVT-III***
Adapted from Dunn & Dunn (1997). *The Peabody Picture Vocabulary Test-III.*

The child is started with vocabulary at his or her present chronological age level and progresses forward until the ceiling level is reached. If the child is not functioning at his or her chronological age level, the assessor moves down a grade level until the child's basal level is found. A raw receptive vocabulary score is calculated and then converted into a standard score. The standard score is then compared with those of a norm-referenced group, yielding an age equivalent score, a percentile and stanine score, along with a normal curve equivalent score. These scores provide the examiner with a strong idea of the child's ability to hear and comprehend spoken vocabulary (listening vocabulary level) as well as providing comparison data on the child's abilities by age level. This is a valuable assessment because it can measure listening vocabulary levels for preschool-aged ELLs as well as adult ELLs. It is also relatively quick and easy to administer. One down side is that it must be given on a one-to-one basis.

The *PPVT-III* is sequential in that it begins with simpler pictures such as those represented in Figure 4.1 and progressively becomes more difficult. The child is started at his or her chronological age level in an attempt to determine a **basal level** and progresses until reaching his or her **ceiling level.**

BASAL LEVEL:
The level at which a person misses 0 or 1—a baseline.

The value in this assessment is that it tests receptive vocabulary and therefore doesn't rely on the student to define or describe the words. Students are able to give the correct number or point to the correct picture when responding to each question. This provides students with a visual support system when taking this assessment, often making it seem much less threatening for them.

CEILING LEVEL:
The level at which a person can go no further—frustration.

Another benefit of using the *PPVT-III* is that it is available in a Spanish-language version called *Test de Vocabulario en Imagenes Peabody (TVIP)* (Dunn, Lugo, Padilla, & Dunn, 1986). This version contains culturally relevant pictures that will enable teachers to develop an accurate picture of the Spanish-speaking ELL's true receptive vocabulary abilities. Often ELLs are thought to be academically deficient or lacking in literacy skills when in reality they are quite proficient in their native languages. Assessments such as the TVIP will allow teachers to be more accurate in their evaluation of ELLs' abilities.

L1:
A term used to signify a person's primary or native language. It literally means "first language."

Oral Language/Vocabulary Assessments

L2:
A term that denotes a person's second language. In this text, L2 refers to the English language.

Oral language/oral vocabulary assessments are more readily available for use with ELLs within the classroom. While some are available in a student's primary language (**L1**), most measure an ELL's English language ability (**L2**). This section will detail those assessments that are for use in a student's primary language (other than English), and then lead into a discussion of assessments available to evaluate an ELL's English oral language/oral vocabulary abilities.

ASSESSMENT OF PRIMARY LANGUAGE ABILITIES

Until recently, most assessments of ELLs were conducted in English only. Although this was valuable, it often left teachers unaware of an ELL's true academic abilities. Teachers may have viewed the student as a *remedial learner* when in fact he or she had several academic strengths that were inaccessible due to a lack of English language proficiency. As educators have become more knowledgeable in teaching ELLs, many have come to understand the need for assessments in multiple languages. This section will begin with more structured, formal assessments and then transition into informal language assessments. The first assessment discussed is called *The Bilingual Verbal Abilities Test (BVAT)* (Munōz-Sandoval, Cummins, Alvado, & Ruef, 1998).

The Bilingual Verbal Abilities Test (BVAT)

The *Bilingual Verbal Abilities Test* or *BVAT* is a test that was developed to assess students in their primary language and a secondary language. It is available in 19 languages, including English. The test is appropriate for ages 5 through adult and takes approximately 30 minutes to administer. The test is comprised of three subtests: verbal analogies, oral vocabulary, and picture vocabulary. A student is first tested in English, and then retested on any "missed" questions in his or her primary language. Because the test requires the administrator to be fluent in both languages, it may be necessary to have two people administer the test or have a bilingual assessor present.

Overall, the test provides teachers with a combined score that shows the student's strengths and needs in dual languages, allowing the student's primary language strengths to become visible. The *BVAT* is administered on a one-to-one basis and will therefore require the teacher to set aside an uninterrupted block of time to conduct the assessment. This assessment can be used to as an entrance and exit exam for various ELD programs as well as a means to determine if special services (gifted or special education) are appropriate for an ELL.

Picture Naming in the Primary Language and Secondary Language

There are two ways to conduct a picture-naming assessment. First, you can purchase a testing kit for the *Expressive One-Word Picture Vocabulary Test (EOWPVT)*. This assessment contains an English and Spanish version within the same kit. In administering the *EOWPVT*, the assessor directs the student to look at a picture or a specific feature within a picture. The student then orally names what the assessor is pointing to in the picture. This assessment varies from the *PPVT* and the *TVIP* in that the student must respond orally. This is an individually administered test that takes 15 to 20 minutes to complete. It is a standardized, norm-referenced test.

A second option that may be more user-friendly for a classroom teacher is to create your own version of the picture naming test. A teacher can collect pictures from a variety of sources that contain culturally relevant items, events, etc. and place them into envelopes. Students can then be asked to orally name features within each picture according to their native language and culture. Envelopes can be developed for each culture within a classroom along with pictures related to the English language environment. Teachers can prepare a standardized list of items to point out and can use the pictures as a means to determine pre- and post-instruction scores as well as language proficiency levels in L1 and L2. It is important not to teach to the test by specifically targeting the pictures but instead engage in language-rich activities that will expand students' vocabularies in many areas.

ASSESSMENT OF ENGLISH LANGUAGE ABILITIES

Many of the assessments discussed in the previous can be used to assess students' primary and secondary language development, thus making it difficult to place them into separate categories. In the next section, the assessments presented will specifically target English language development and proficiency. Again, I will begin by addressing more formal assessments and then graduate into informal and more inexpensive assessments. These do not need to be given to all students; it is important to select those that you find to be most useful and practical in your specific circumstances.

Idea Oral Proficiency Test (IPT-O)

The *Idea Oral Proficiency Test* or *IPT-O* (Williams, Ballard, Tighe, Dalton, & Amori, 1991) is commonly given to identify an ELL's level of oral language proficiency in English. Because it is a standardized test, it is often given as a means of placing students into the appropriate classroom educational setting by identifying them as either Limited English Proficient (LEP) or Non-Limited English Proficient (NLEP). This test can be given to an individual or small group of students, making it more manageable for a classroom setting.

Basic Inventory of Natural Language (BINL)

The *Basic Inventory of Natural Language (BINL)* (Herbert, 1979, 1983) has been used for several years as a test to assess language dominance and proficiency levels in English and Spanish. While it does address oral language ability, it also measures proficiency in reading and other areas of language arts.

Listen Up Skills Assessment

The *Listen Up Skills Assessment* (Watson & Barker, 1995) is a relatively new assessment that has been developed to assess a student's ability to follow a series of directions, comprehend oral stories and lessons, and interpret oral information. This assessment can be given to English-only students and ELLs.

Oral Language Usage Observations: Ethnographic Field Notes

Collecting observational data as a form of assessment can be quite powerful when certain conditions are met. According to Johnston (1997), one of the requirements of observation is that the observer be quite knowledgeable about the "domain to be assessed" (p. 11). In this case the domain refers to the area of language arts that is to be observed—oral language. While this may seem like common sense, it is imperative that the assessor understand the content of the domain as well as the steps necessary to acquire proficiency in the area. In other words, to accurately observe English language acquisition by an ELL, a teacher must understand all of the stages involved in the process. Without this knowledge, errors in interpretation of the observations can result.

There are many formats for conducting observations—some are more formal as in the use of a checklist, while others involve the collection of anecdotal notes. The use of a systematic format for recording notes has been developed by Carolyn Frank (1999) in her book *Ethnographic Eyes*. Frank suggests that teachers collect ethnographic field notes in a two-step process that she calls, "note taking" and "note making" (see Figure 4.2).

While observing a student using oral language within a given context, the teacher jots down notes in the "note taking" column. The notes generally take two forms: direct quotes by the students and notes documenting activities, materials, and movements occurring during the observation. It is important to directly quote the student being observed in order to develop a clear picture of his or her true language abilities in L1

FIGURE 4.2 Sample Ethnographic Note-Taking Form

Note Taking	Note Making

Adapted from: Frank, C. (1999). *Ethnographic eyes: A teacher's guide to classroom observation.* Portsmouth, NH: Heinemann.

and L2. Frank (1999) emphasizes the fact that the teacher is *not* to make any judgments during the note-taking phase. When judgments are made at this point, they can color what is being observed, in either a positive or negative fashion.

After the observation is complete, the observer will want to let the notes sit for a short period of time. When coming back to the notes, the teacher can then jot down comments or questions in the "note making" column. It is then necessary to share with the student the notes being made during the observation along with the comments and questions made subsequent to the observation. This step allows the observer to confirm or disprove his or her initial judgments and gain a more balanced perspective. The observational notes and the conference notes can be dated and placed in the student's portfolio, adding to the data yielded through a variety of assessments. These notes become a tool to document the ELL's language growth across time.

In addition to the assessments discussed above, teachers can accurately assess a student's primary and secondary language abilities using the Language Experience Approach (LEA). While LEA has often been used in primary classrooms as a teaching strategy, it has also proven to be an excellent assessment tool (Nessell, 1981). The LEA is based on the idea of asking young students to dictate a story while the teacher transcribes the story onto a piece of paper. What distinguishes LEA from a simple dictation task is that it is done in a more systematic fashion.

In the Language Experience Approach the teacher begins with a stimulus. The stimulus can be an object (such as a stuffed animal for younger children or a telescope for more advanced students who are acquiring English), a picture, a story, music, or some other type of conversation starter. Together, the teacher and students discuss the stimulus object in an attempt to generate interesting ideas for writing. Either in a small group, whole group, or an individual setting, the students dictate a story as the teacher writes it on chart paper. Together they practice reading the story aloud until the students are comfortable with the story vocabulary and can read it fluently and with proper intonation.

WORD SORTS:
Learners are given a series of words printed on small cards or slips of paper and are asked to place them into categories. These categories can be teacher selected (closed sorts), or they may be learner selected (open sorts). After sorting the words, the learners are asked to justify the choices made when sorting the words.

Using the dictated story, the teacher transfers the story from the chart paper into a blank book. Students are encouraged to illustrate the books, which will subsequently become their reading text. The idea behind the use of such dictated texts is that the students can more easily learn to read stories that are written in their own words. As the students progress, the teacher will be able to note the qualitative differences in the dictated stories they are producing.

Additionally, teachers can pull spelling words from the stories to use for individual and/or group spelling instruction. These words can be studied and manipulated using open and closed **word sorts**. In an *open sort* the students can sort the words into their own categories. In a *closed sort,* the students are asked to sort the words according to predetermined categories provided by the teacher. For example, the teacher could ask the students to sort the words into piles based on whether they have a long or short vowel sound or by their part of speech (nouns, verbs, adjectives, etc.). It is important to have students read the words from each pile to the teacher or to a peer and describe why they sorted the words into those specific piles. It is through the use of questioning and conversation that the teacher will be able to note increases in the students' oral vocabulary level while also teaching them a variety of other valuable skills and concepts. Together, the informal and formal assessments described above will provide teachers with substantial information regarding the abilities of the ELLs in English and their primary language.

Evaluating Assessment Results

After selecting and administering the appropriate oral language/vocabulary assessments, it is time to pull together all of the data collected and begin to evaluate the findings. Rather than just focusing on numerical scores, it is valuable to begin to make a simple *strengths and needs chart* based on the findings. This can be written out on an index card and placed in the student's portfolio. Additional cards may be added as the student progresses through the school year. Keeping each of the cards rather than revising one card allows the teacher to have a visual record of the progress made by the student across time (see Figure 4.3).

FIGURE 4.3   Strengths and Needs Chart: Anecdotal Notes Used When Evaluating Assessment Results

Samantha's Assessments:

TVIP: October 23rd

- 8th stanine

PPVT-III: October 24th

- 3rd stanine

Strengths:

- High level of listening vocabulary in spanish!
- Knew everyday vocabulary as well as more technical content area vocabulary

Needs:

- Increase oral and listening vocabulary in English—start with everyday language and also introduce some content area vocabulary

*** I need to find out her reading level in Spanish, as well as her abilities to write in Spanish. She really seems strong in the language arts.

For example, if a student, Samantha, scores in the 3rd stanine on the *PPVT-III* but scores in the 8th stanine on the *TVIP*, you have gleaned some powerful information that can be used when developing an instructional plan for the student. In this case, Samantha has shown that she has an above average level of listening vocabulary in Spanish, which is her primary language. When tested in English though, Samantha scores well below average indicating that she has a strong language foundation in her primary language but needs more exposure to English language vocabulary. The assessment has made visible the fact that Samantha has a high degree of potential in this particular area of language arts.

Based on your evaluation of Samantha's strengths and needs, you can begin to select strategies to enhance her English language listening and oral language vocabulary. Below is a list of instructional strategies that may prove beneficial for Samantha or any other student needing support with English language development.

Strategies Promoting English Language Listening and Oral Vocabulary Development

- Daily read-alouds from a variety of texts and textual genres.
- Grand conversations and instructional conversations.
- Cooperative group activities across the curriculum.
- Multimedia lessons incorporating audiotapes, movies, plays, reader's theater, and other language-based activities.
- Language Experience Approach.
- Literature Circles in primary and secondary languages.
- Direct Experience Approach.
- Reciprocal teaching.
- Choral reading, shared reading, and assisted reading.

Many strategies can be embedded within the context of the classroom on a daily basis to improve the vocabulary level of ELLs and English-only students. Listening and oral vocabulary are the cornerstones of language acquisition and also lay the foundation for reading comprehension and written language proficiency. By providing ELLs with a language-rich classroom environment, teachers can increase the students' overall academic achievement while providing them with the tools to communicate effectively within the outside community. Therefore, accurate assessment, evaluation, and the implementation of relevant strategy instruction is essential.

Spend a few minutes reviewing the statements presented in the Chapter Anticipation Guide at the beginning of the chapter. Compare your notes with those **highlighted.**

End-of-the-Chapter Anticipation Guide

Agree	Disagree	Statement
✗		Vocabulary instruction is divided into two distinct parts: receptive vocabulary and expressive vocabulary. *True—Receptive vocabulary relates to the vocabulary needed to read and listen while expressive vocabulary relates to the vocabulary needed to speak and write. The two types of vocabulary exist in both a primary and secondary language.*
✗		ELLs go through several phases of language development. The first phase is the silent phase in which they listen and do not respond. *True—It is important to understand that ELLs spend the first six to nine months in the silent phase of language acquisition. During this stage, ELLs listen to the language in an attempt to make sense of it and to acquire new vocabulary before trying to speak the language themselves. It is a time when they need to listen in order to learn. It allows the ELL to learn in a risk-free environment.*
	✗	Most children acquire approximately 500 new vocabulary words per year prior to entering kindergarten. *False—Most children have a listening and speaking vocabulary of up to 10,000 words by the time they enter kindergarten. This means that children learn up to 2,000 new words per year prior to beginning school. This is an amazing bit of information!*
✗		The ability to listen to language is related to a person's ability to acquire vocabulary in his or her primary and secondary languages. *True—Listening is an essential, yet often overlooked skill in second language acquisition. It is through listening that a person begins to understand the flow of language, the multiple meanings of words and phrases, and the specific nuances of a particular language.*

ASSESSMENT *TOOLKIT*

Oral Language and Listening Vocabulary

- *Bilingual Verbal Abilities Test (BVAT)* and
- *Peabody Picture Vocabulary Test-III (PPVT-III)*; *Test de Vocabulario Imagenes Peabody (TVIP)* or
- *Expressive One-Word Picture Vocabulary Test (EOWPVT)*
- Journal for the collection of anecdotal notes, ethnographic field notes
- Copies of dictated stories for students obtained during the Language Experience Approach (LEA) that have been placed in the student's portfolio
- Blank audiotapes and tape recorder
- Variety of pictures from magazines, books, etc. to be used in assessing the student in primary and secondary languages
- Student portfolios

CHAPTER FIVE

Reading Acquisition in the Primary and Secondary Languages

Read through each of the following statements prior to reading the chapter. Place a checkmark in either the box labeled "agree" or "disagree" depending upon whether you believe the statement to be true or false. As you read the chapter, refer back to the chart and confirm or modify your initial responses.

Initial Chapter Anticipation Guide

Agree	Disagree	Statement
		Reading and writing development in English as a second language is essentially the same as when learning to read and write in one's primary language.
		There are four main cueing systems that help a reader to make sense of a text: pragmatic, graphophonic, semantic, and syntactic.
		The model utilized to teach children to speak a primary or secondary language has little impact on the type of reading and writing instruction provided in schools.
		Reading and writing are interrelated developmental processes that are linear in nature.
		Students who learn to read in their primary language first have a smoother transition when learning to read in a second language.

TEACHER *VIGNETTE*

During a recent school year, a new student arrived in my fifth grade classroom during the sixth week of school. According to his mother, he had attended kindergarten and first grade in Mexico and had gone to school in the United States for grades 2 through 4. Marco's oral English vocabulary was at a fifth-grade level, and he appeared, at first glance, to have strong language skills. After working with Marco for a few weeks, I soon realized he was greatly struggling with both reading and writing in English.

Each day when the children arrived at school, they spent the first 15 minutes writing in their journals. I had a topic posted on the board for them to write about, or they had the option of selecting their own topic. Marco was quite conscientious about writing for the entire 15 minutes. In fact, he often filled two pages of his journal. After writing, the students were encouraged to share their writing with a partner. Marco seemed quite comfortable sharing his writing and often volunteered to share it with the entire class.

As a part of my classroom routine, I collect and respond to one set of journals each evening, generally collecting them from one collaborative group at a time. Within this time frame I am able to read everyone's journal every two weeks. At the end of the second week, I sat down to read Marco's journal and was stunned at what I saw on each page. Marco had strung together a series of letters, in a seemingly random order, neglecting to leave space between his words. Within his writing I was able to read one or two words that he had written conventionally, but the rest of the writing was indecipherable. Having taught both primary and intermediate grades, I had become rather proficient at reading phonetic spelling, but in Marco's case, the writing was not based on sound-symbol correspondences in English or Spanish. At that point, I was unsure of how to proceed.

Janet, 5ᵗʰ grade teacher
Los Angeles, California

I first met Janet in a university reading center where she was taking courses to obtain a reading specialist credential. One of the driving forces behind her continuing education rested on her desire to help students like Marco. Although he was not the first student in a similar situation, Janet hoped she would be able to provide him with more help than she had in the past. Janet wanted to better understand reading and language acquisition so she would be able to reach her students. Marco exhibited a great deal of motivation to learn to read and write proficiently and mimicked those behaviors he saw demonstrated by fluent readers and writers. Janet put a great deal of effort into researching second language reading acquisition in her journey toward becoming a proficient teacher of ELLs. Janet went back to many of the reading methods texts she had used in her teacher education program to build a more solid foundation in the teaching of reading. This is where we will begin our journey as well. In order to help students in learning to read English in first grade, fifth grade, or eighth grade it is important to understand the theoretical foundations and developmental stages of reading and writing.

Theories of Reading Acquisition

Often referred to as the "Reading Wars" of late, there are several overlapping and sometimes conflicting theories of reading acquisition and instruction. Depending on the theory of instruction adopted by a teacher, school, or school district, the impact of a theoretical orientation is tremendous for students, especially for second language students. Durkin (1995) addressed this issue when she discussed the various theories of language acquisition in her book, *Language Issues: Readings for Teachers.* Durkin stated that the model utilized to teach children to speak a primary or secondary language has an impact on the type of reading and writing instruction provided in schools. Therefore, if schools adopt a more behaviorist view of language acquisition, the curriculum will tend to support these principles versus if a more constructivist approach has been adopted. In other words, the curriculum will be more reflective of a skills-based model with long periods of drill and practice as compared to a school that adopts a more social constructivist model of language acquisition. Regardless of the model adopted, reading theorists agree that extensive reading is essential for the development of reading comprehension (Cummins, 2005, p. 8).

Figure 5.1 presents the three main theories of reading acquisition prevalent in the research literature. The graphic attempts to combine the reading theories continuum into a more integrated approach that considers each of the models in a dynamic structure leading to a fourth approach that utilizes components from each of the models. The end goal is to provide students with the most comprehensive instructional program available in order to gain meaning from a text (Pearson, 2000).

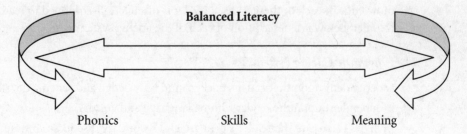

FIGURE 5.1 Cyclical Melding of Reading Instruction Models

By taking an integrated approach to the teaching of reading, a teacher is more likely to find the most appropriate method for teaching students based on their individual strengths and needs, thus eliminating the need to make a child change to fit a particular methodology. It is important to teach the child rather than trying to conform to a predetermined curriculum or approach. This becomes particularly important when working with ELLs because they have often experienced a mismatch between their academic needs and strengths and methods of English language instruction. In order to better understand the processes involved in learning to read, it becomes necessary to clearly define reading and develop an awareness of the complexities involved.

The Processes Involved in Reading Fluently

DEFINING READING

Reading involves making sense from a printed text through the use of the graphophonic, semantic, syntactic, and pragmatic cueing systems. Each cueing system lends support to the reader as he or she attempts to make meaning from the words on the page. Proficient readers are able to balance each of the systems in an integrated fashion that minimizes any disruption to fluency, and in turn, to comprehension. Therefore, it is the interaction between the text and the reader that leads to true comprehension (Brantley, 2004; Goodman, 1986; Tompkins, 2001).

CUEING SYSTEM:
A system of language that allows us to communicate both orally and in writing. Each system provides us with a different type of information.

Figure 5.2 demonstrates the overlapping nature of the **cueing systems** involved in the reading process. Each cueing system is interdependent upon the others. If a child relies too heavily on just one system, it may hinder his or her ability to decode and subsequently to comprehend a text. By teaching strategies to develop each of the four cueing systems, a child is more likely to become a proficient reader.

Each of the four cueing systems is interconnected, and all four systems work together to help a reader to make sense of a text. It is through the use of these cueing systems that a reader is able to decode the print, bring background knowledge to the text, and understand what he or she has read. Without strategy knowledge in each of these areas, a reader is often left ill-equipped to read.

Detailed below is a description of each of the cueing systems.

The Pragmatic Cueing System

- Is dependent upon the reader's background knowledge and schema development.
- Is dependent upon the reader's home language and culture.
- Involves the use of the reader's primary and secondary discourse communities.
- Is context-dependent.

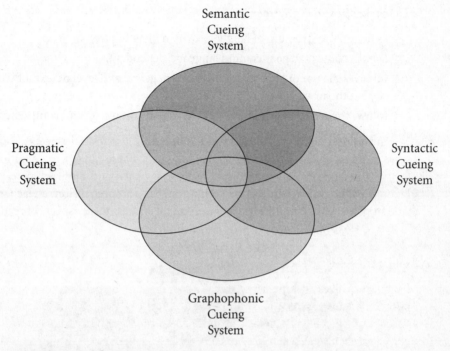

FIGURE 5.2   The Four Cueing Systems
Adapted from Goodman, 1986; Tompkins, 2001.

The Semantic Cueing System

- Allows the reader to make sense of a text.
- Relies on a reader's background knowledge and schema development.
- Is both context-dependent and reader-dependent.
- Relies on meaning cues within the text: pictures, sentence structure, context clues, etc.
- Allows the reader to make self-corrections to increase text comprehension.

The Graphophonic Cueing System

- Allows the reader to use sound/symbol correspondences to decode print.
- Relies on visual cues.
- Utilizes such strategies as chunking, blending, and breaking words into component parts in order to decode text.
- Is based on a 1:1 correspondence between print and letter sounds.

The Syntactic Cueing System

- Relies on the structure of language to gain meaning from a text.
- Is both context-dependent and language-dependent.
- Involves the use of grammar, punctuation, genre, and level of text difficulty to decode at the word, sentence, and paragraph levels.
- Allows the reader to gain fluency (prosody, reading rate, and comprehension).

In addition to the four cueing systems, there are also several aspects of reading that serve to impact a child's comprehension of a text. These range from emotional or affective aspects to such physiological aspects as visual and auditory perception (see Figure 5.3). By understanding the complexities of comprehension, a teacher can provide students with a multitude of strategies that address these aspects of reading.

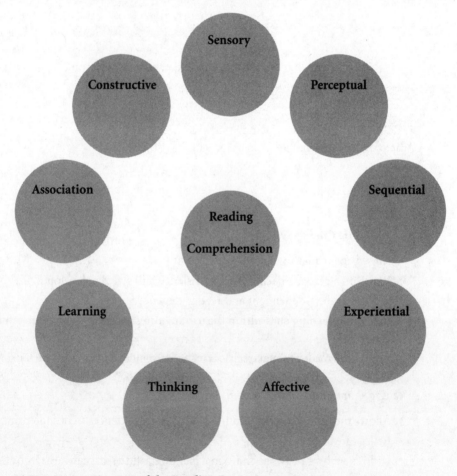

FIGURE 5.3   Aspects of the Reading Process
Adapted from Burns, Roe, & Ross, 1999.

SENSORY AND PERCEPTUAL ASPECTS

Reading comprehension involves a complex set of interrelated abilities that impact a reader's decoding of words and understanding of a text. The first two aspects of comprehension are physiologically based: sensory aspects and perceptual aspects. Within the category of sensory aspects are visual and sound acuity.

VISUAL ACUITY:
The ability to distinguish visual images of varying sizes, shapes, colors, and contrasts at different distances. It also refers to the eyes' ability to work together to see clearly.

Visual acuity can be measured using such devices as the *Keystone Telebinocular Visual Survey*, which assesses near and far vision, convergence and fusion, the ability to distinguish colors, and depth perception. This is more complex than most vision screenings routinely performed at a school site. Most schools generally test distance visual acuity rather than some of the more complex skills needed for reading.

HEARING ACUITY:
The ability to distinguish and hear sounds of varying decibel or intensity levels and at different frequencies. A deficit in either area may result in a hearing loss (Gunning, 2002).

Hearing acuity can be measured by using a standard hearing instrument called an audiometer that assesses the ability to hear sounds at different frequencies and decibel levels. Most elementary schools perform hearing screenings in the primary grades. While these are beneficial, they may fail to detect a hearing deficit due to outside noise interference when conducting the test. If you suspect a hearing problem, it may be best to refer the child to a specialist or ask the school nurse to redo the test in a quiet environment.

The first of the perceptual aspects of reading comprehension relates to the reader's ability to visually discriminate between individual letters and words. A reader must be able to differentiate between each letter in order to appropriately decode a word.

The second aspect involves a reader's ability to develop phonological awareness (Adams, 2001; Goswami, 2000, 2001) or auditory discrimination skills. Reutzel and Cooter (2003) define phonological awareness as "the understanding that spoken language is composed of smaller units such as *phrases, words, syllables, onsets, rimes,* and *phonemes*" (p. 171). It is this ability that allows the reader to break words into meaningful units to decode words and build comprehension.

SEQUENTIAL AND EXPERIENTIAL ASPECTS

The *sequential aspects* of comprehension are often referred to as the concepts of print. Marie Clay (1991) states that children exhibit "orienting behaviors" that are mastered over time. It is these behaviors that are visible when assessing a learner's understanding of the concepts of print. The orienting behaviors have the following components: "(a) a movement-in-space or motor component, (b) a visual perception or looking component, and (c) a mental or cognitive component" (p. 148).

When observing the learner to determine his or her level of mastery of the sequential aspects of comprehension, a teacher will look for the learner's ability to track print in a left-to-right and top-to-bottom motion. It is also necessary to ascertain whether the learner understands that oral and written language are strung together in a sequen-

Teachers can assess a student's level of background knowledge about a text through the use of picture walks and book conversations prior to reading the text.

tial manner based on the rules of grammar and syntax. These rules will vary depending upon the learner's primary language. Because of this, teachers would benefit from understanding the nuances of the learner's home language. It would also help to clarify some misconceptions that may arise as the learner acquires a second language.

Strategies

Listed below are instructional strategies that can be used to promote the sequential aspects of reading:

- Choral reading
- Echo reading
- Reader's theater
- Poetry
- Reading old familiars

The *experiential aspects* of comprehension are related to the reader's own cognitive schemas. Within this construct, readers utilize their background knowledge and experiences to form and build upon schemas of information. Schema theory was first proposed by Rumelhart (1980) where he described specific structures of knowledge that form in the mind called *schemata*. The schemata are made up of the reader's background knowledge and experiences and are organized in meaningful structures. It is the brain's way of filing information on related topics in such a way as to make it accessible as needed.

Strategies

Listed below are instructional strategies that can be implemented to promote the experiential aspects of reading:

- K-W-L
- Predictions prior to reading
- Directed Reading-Thinking Activity (DRTA)
- Directed Listening-Thinking Activity (DLTA)
- Graphic organizers
- Sketch to Stretch

THINKING AND LEARNING ASPECTS

Reading is a meaning-making activity requiring the reader to draw upon many sources of information to understand a text. The *thinking aspects* of reading comprehension require the reader to interpret the graphic symbols on the page simultaneously while using the graphophonic, pragmatic, semantic, and syntactic cueing systems. Not only are readers required to interpret what is written on the page, they must be able to infer meanings not specifically stated by the author. This ability requires them to read critically and look for what is visible and what is invisible.

Strategies

Listed below are instructional strategies that can be implemented to promote the thinking aspects of reading:

- Oral retellings
- Directed Reading-Thinking Activity (DRTA)
- Directed Listening-Thinking Activity (DLTA)
- Question-Answer Relationships (QAR)
- Guided reading at the instructional level
- Reciprocal teaching

In order coordinate the complex processes involved in comprehension, readers must be taught explicit strategies for reading a variety of texts. It is through the *learning aspect* of comprehension that teachers provide strategy instruction through a system of scaffolded instruction. Factors such as the time spent engaged in instruction, time spent practicing literacy strategies, and the reader's motivation to read all impact the learning aspect of comprehension.

Strategies

Listed below are instructional strategies that can be implemented to promote the learning aspects of reading:

- Reading a variety of materials based on the reader's interests
- Survey-Question-Read-Recite-Revise (SQ3R)
- Guided reading/mini-lessons
- Readers' workshop
- Rereading old familiars

ASSOCIATIVE AND CONSTRUCTIVE ASPECTS

The final two aspects of reading comprehension are the associative and constructive aspects. The *associative aspect* relates to the reader's ability to associate letter sounds to letters within a word. This aspect is closely tied to both auditory and visual perception but also considers the ability to put the letters and sounds into meaningful units such as words, sentences, and paragraphs.

Strategies

Listed below are instructional strategies used to promote the associative aspects of reading:

- Letter, picture, and word sorts
- Making words
- Language Experience Approach (LEA)
- Reader response activities
- Literature logs

The *constructive aspect* involves the reader in a continual cycle of constructing and reconstructing meaning when reading. This reconstructive process is influenced by the experiences brought to a text by the reader, by the author's choice of vocabulary, by the feelings elicited while reading a text, and by social interactions with other readers. The constructive aspect is dynamic and nonlinear. It ensues throughout a text and may continue to occur as the reader engages in response activities meant to extend understanding. It was best summed up in the following quote by Constance Weaver: "Reading is seldom a solitary act" (Weaver, 1994, p.31).

Strategies

Listed below are instructional strategies used to promote the constructive aspects of reading:

- Dialogue journals
- Predictions/read to confirm or disprove/new predictions
- Literature circles
- Reader's workshop
- Writer's workshop
- Sketch to Stretch

All of the strategies discussed in the previous pages can be implemented throughout the reading and writing process depending upon the reader's needs, interests, and strengths. They may be modified to be developmentally appropriate. In the next section, the stages of the reading process will be discussed in detail.

Stages of the Reading Process

Varying theories of reading development have been proposed over the years. While the names may have changed for the stages readers progress through as they develop fluent reading capabilities, the basic dimensions have remained stable. In order to develop a common language when referring to reading acquisition, this text will be based on the stages developed by Marie Clay (1991) and Fountas and Pinnell (2001). In their work, they have noted five main stages of literacy development that relate to both reading and writing.

EMERGENT READERS

Emergent readers generally range in age from 2 to 7 years old. They are beginning to familiarize themselves with the concepts of print related to directionality, one-to-one correspondence between the spoken and written word, and the value of picture clues to the meaning of a story. They may also develop an understanding that the printed word carries the main meaning of a story. Emergent readers begin to make text-to-world connections and may be able to extend upon what is written on the page.

EARLY READERS

Building upon the concepts attained as an emergent reader, early readers now begin to rely more heavily on the printed text than on the pictures in a book. Often they are beginning to develop word recognition strategies such as "monitoring, searching, cross-checking, and self-correction" (Fountas & Pinnell, 1996, p. 178). Early readers also begin to develop a bank of sight words that allows them to read with increased speed as they are reading more often in phrases rather than single words. As a general rule, early readers are between the ages of 5 and 7. Because readers develop at varying rates, a teacher may have a class containing both emergent and early readers as well as readers in the next developmental stage, the transitional reader.

TRANSITIONAL READERS

Transitional readers are making the leap into fluent reading as they are generally able to read in meaningful phrases with a comfortable pace and appropriate voice intonation. They are able to integrate the four cueing systems into their reading with little disruption to meaning and flow. Transitional readers are able to read more lengthy texts with little reliance on pictures for text meaning. Again, these readers tend to range in age from 5 to 7 years.

SELF-EXTENDING READERS

In the fourth developmental stage, readers are progressing into reading independence. They often read a variety of textual genres and use reading as a tool for gaining new knowledge or building upon existing knowledge. Self-extending readers are able to read more complex texts and are beginning to read for a variety of purposes. Often these readers range in age from 6 to 9 years of age.

ADVANCED READERS

Readers categorized as advanced readers are those readers who have attained a level of mastery with reading. They are generally over the age of 9 and have become proficient, reading and comprehending various text sources. Advanced readers enjoy reading and use reading as a means of gaining knowledge. They read fluently and can interpret texts at both a concrete and inferential level. Advanced readers connect what they've read to themselves to other texts and to the world around them. They have internalized a series of reading strategies that are used interchangeably as they read different texts. The goal in teaching reading is to help all students become advanced readers and for ELLs to become advanced readers in their primary and secondary languages. So how does a teacher guide a learner through the various stages of reading development in both languages? The remainder of the chapter will discuss second language reading acquisition and how it relates to primary language reading acquisition.

Second Language Reading Acquisition: Reading in English

Does the process of learning to read English as a second language differ from learning to read in another language? If so, how does it differ? In the final section of the chapter, we'll delve into learning to read English as a second language, all the while considering the home language the reader brings to the process.

Within the research literature regarding literacy development in a second language, two main views have emerged. The first view is called the *word recognition view* in which reading is "primarily a process of recognizing words" (Freeman & Freeman, 2005, p. 36). Within this construct, readers begin to develop an ever-growing sight word vocabulary through various prereading activities. Readers are taught word attack skills based on phonics rules and syllabication as the main strategies for decoding unknown words. Oral reading tends to be the main form of assessing a reader's vocabulary development and strategy use within this model.

Another theory of literacy development in a second language has also been prevalent in the current literacy research. The *socio-psycholinguistic view* is meaning-based and states that readers use their background knowledge, experiences, and the four cueing systems to read. Readers acquire new vocabulary through wide reading of a variety of texts and textual genres and studying word parts as a means to understand a text (Freeman & Freeman, 2005).

Depending upon the view prescribed to by a teacher, school, or district, reading proficiency will be defined differently. Even though this may be the case, the research is quite clear in regard to the qualities that are demonstrated by good readers.

WHAT CHARACTERIZES A GOOD READER?

To begin the conversation about the qualities of a good reader, think about the strategies you employ when reading a novel, a newspaper article, and an unfamiliar content area text. Do you read each of these texts the same way and at the same speed? What differences and similarities do you notice? Much research has been done to delineate the qualities of a good reader in the hopes of being able to teach these qualities or strategies to novice and struggling readers.

One of the first qualities a good reader exhibits is the ability to set a purpose when reading. Here the reader takes note of the type of specific textual qualities and content by previewing it. It is through the preview process that the reader develops a purpose for reading and well as the motivation to read the text (Ellery, 2005).

Closely related to setting a purpose, readers will bring some background knowledge and experiences to the new text to help them to understand what they're reading (Anderson, 1994). Good readers have learned strategies that enable them to access their background knowledge and determine what is useful and where gaps may exist in their knowledge base. Some of the strategies used are (a) visualization; (b) generating predictions based on the title and pictures in a text; and (c) developing questions before, during, and after reading (Peregoy & Boyle, 2005). These strategies are intermingled and often used without the reader's conscious awareness. The more one reads, the more these strategies become internalized.

Along with these qualities is readers' ability to visually process print and then interpret what they've read. The process of interpretation requires the reader to under-

Good readers are actively engaged in the reading process, which promotes comprehension, enjoyment, and confidence.

stand various text structures, vocabulary, and "sentence signals" (Peregoy & Boyle, 2005, p. 19). *Sentence signals* are phrases that give readers a signal about what is coming up in the text and clarifies the genre and structure of the text they are engaged in reading. "Once upon a time" and "First, we are going to describe the processes involved . . ." are examples of sentence signals that good readers automatically key into as they read.

Good readers also use context to help them to understand the meaning of a text. They tend to use the context to "interpret words and sentences" rather than to decode individual words (Perfetti, 2005, p. 12). Less skilled readers rely more on context as a means of identifying words, often failing to understand the words they are reading.

Additionally, good readers are known to be strategic readers. Strategic readers continually audit their comprehension of a text by rereading sections, confirming or disproving initial predictions, and modifying the questions they are asking (Brown, Campione, & Day, 1981). This process is complex and requires the reader to be actively engaged in the reading process. Together, all of these qualities allow a good reader to read fluently and with a high level of understanding. Now, what is the likelihood that these qualities will transfer from a reader's primary language to the new language he or she is acquiring?

DOES LITERACY LEARNING TRANSFER FROM A PRIMARY TO A SECONDARY LANGUAGE?

"The transfer of literacy ability from one language to another depends on similarities and differences between their writing systems, including the unit of speech symbolized by each character" (Peregoy & Boyle, 2005, p. 22). This refers to the type of symbol used within a particular language system (alphabetic, syllabic, or logographic) and the concepts of print (directionality, spacing, etc.) within the system. Therefore, if the two languages systems are fairly consistent, the transfer of literacy ability will take place more easily for the learner. This is further contingent upon the learner's level of competence in reading, writing, and oral language within his or her primary language. The higher the level of competence, the more likely he or she is to transfer literacy abilities to a new language.

WHAT IS THE BEST WAY TO TEACH READING IN A SECOND LANGUAGE?

Another approach to the acquisition of reading in a new language is based on Cunningham's (1995) Four Blocks Model of Reading Development, composed of (a) guided reading, (b) independent reading, (c) word work, and (d) writing. In addition to these components, daily instructional time must be allocated for the addition of an English Language Development (ELD) component (García & Beltrán, 2005). This is especially true for those students attending school in states that have endorsed English immersion programs for ELLs.

García and Beltrán (2005) have described the essential elements of a quality ELD program that will lay the foundation for the academic success of all ELLs. While there are many valuable teaching strategies that can be built into this component, the main strategies will be addressed throughout the remainder of the chapter. To begin with, it is imperative that ELLs be instructed through the use of quality literature. Such literature provides an exemplary model of the English language while also captivating the readers with meaningful and appealing stories. It is also possible to select relevant cultural models throughout the literature.

Teachers should also select cognitive strategies that provide ELLs with a sound educational program. These strategies are best if contextually situated and rich in language usage. Academic and conversational vocabulary instruction is another valuable aspect of the ELD block of literacy learning. Teacher demonstrations, repetition, and collaborative learning experiences all promote the acquisition of vocabulary, reading, writing, and speaking in a second language. The use of various media will also serve to enhance the ELD literacy lessons by activating and building upon the readers' prior experiences while also allowing them multiple ways to express what they've learned.

Clearly, the fifth block should consist of authentic, scaffolded, meaning-based learning experiences in which the learners have time to work with the teacher, collaboratively with their peers, and independently. Together, the Five Blocks Model of Literacy Instruction will provide ELLs with the greatest chance of academic success (García & Beltrán, 2005).

Spend a few minutes reviewing the statements presented in the Chapter Anticipation Guide at the beginning of the chapter. Compare your notes with those **highlighted.**

End-of-the-Chapter Anticipation Guide

Agree	Disagree	Statement
✗		Reading and writing development in English as a second language is essentially the same as when learning to read and write in one's primary language. *True—Overall, the reading and writing processes involved in learning a new language are the same. All languages are built on learning a set of symbols (alphabetic or characters) and making meaning from them based on prior knowledge and an interaction with the text. While the symbols may vary, the cognitive processes are essentially the same.*
✗		There are four main cueing systems that help a reader to make sense of a text: pragmatic, graphophonic, semantic, and syntactic. *True—In order to read fluently and comprehend different texts, readers use the four cueing systems interchangeably as they read.*
	✗	The model utilized to teach children to speak a primary or secondary language has little impact on the type of reading and writing instruction provided in schools. *False—The reading model or theoretical orientation of a particular school, district, or teacher has a tremendous impact on the teaching strategies, texts, and assessments utilized to teach all students. This is often evidenced by the types of reading programs adopted by a state and its schools. In particular, assessment systems are heavily influenced by the reading model in place. For example, standardized tests are more representative of the decoding and skills model of reading.*

	✘	Reading and writing are interrelated developmental process-es that are linear in nature. *False—While reading and writing are interrelated developmental processes, neither is a linear process. Readers and writers continually move back and forth within the processes as needed to read, write, and comprehend a piece of text thus making the process recursive.*
✘		Students who learn to read in their primary language first have a smoother transition when learning to read in a second language. *True—Overall, students tend to acquire a second language more easily when they are fluent in their native language. This is true because they have developed an understanding of the processes involved in learning to read unknown words based on the semantic, syntactic, and graphophonemic structures of their first language. These skills can then be transferred to their new learning in English. The more closely related the structures of the first language, the easier the acquisition of the second language becomes for the reader.*

Assessment and Development of the Concepts of Print, Phonemic Awareness, and the Alphabetic Principle

CHAPTER ANTICIPATION GUIDE

Read through each of the following statements prior to reading the chapter. Place a checkmark in either the box labeled "agree" or "disagree" depending upon whether you believe the statement to be true or false. As you read the chapter, refer back to the chart and confirm or modify your initial responses.

Initial Chapter Anticipation Guide

Agree	Disagree	Statement
		ELLs can transfer skills and concepts learned in their primary language into English.
		Marie Clay's *Observation Survey* was intended to be used as a readiness assessment for teachers.
		Phonics and *phonemic awareness* are essentially interchangeable terms.
		The use of daily read-alouds promotes the development of emergent and early reading skills and concepts for ELLs of all ages.
		ELLs must have mastered the concepts of print and the alphabetic principle and have demonstrated a high degree of phonemic awareness prior to being exposed to authentic texts and other reading material.

TEACHER *VIGNETTE*

Manuel was in the sixth grade when his family relocated to the northwestern region of the United States. Having learned to read, speak, and write in Spanish at a very early age, he was a confident student in his home country of Guatemala. When he walked into his new middle school classroom, however, Manuel was suddenly terrified. As he looked around the room, he saw few students who resembled him and the friends he had left behind. While everyone smiled at him and spoke to him, Manuel had the urge to flee. Overwhelmed by the sounds of this new language, Manuel hurried to his assigned seat and put his head down on his desk.

He pretty much remained in this same stance for the first week of school until he began to single out familiar sounds in this new language. Also, he began to understand words that he found to be very similar to words in his own language. Excited about finally making sense of some of what he was hearing, Manuel asked his mother to take him to the library. He selected easy books that contained pictures so he could begin to associate the new English vocabulary words with the pictures in the books. Using his strong ability to sound out words, he was quickly able to learn to read and understand these books. Within six months, Manuel was reading books at a much higher level. His teacher worked with him to increase his vocabulary and provided him with a variety of visual aids to increase his understanding of what was taking place around him.

By the end of sixth grade, Manuel was gaining confidence in his academic abilities and had made many new friends along the way. It was interesting to listen to him talk to his friends because he had picked up English slang in no time.

Though the transition was not an easy one for him, Manuel was successful in bringing his strong Spanish language skills into play as he acquired English. Without his successful academic career in Guatemala, it may have taken Manuel years to learn to read, speak, and write in English. These would then have been years in which he fell behind his peers in the content areas of science, social studies, and possibly mathematics.

Manuel 2005

Defining and Assessing the Concepts of Print, Phonemic Awareness, and the English Language Alphabetic Principle

In the emergent stage of reading development, children are exposed to print in a variety of settings and for a variety of purposes. They begin to listen and follow along as their parents or others read to them. They begin to develop an understanding of directionality, both in the sense that print is read from left to right and from top to bottom. Children also notice that the pictures and text have meaning, and they may start to memorize their favorite books, all the while mimicking the proficient readers that they have been listening to and reading with since birth. Children begin to notice print in their environment and may begin to recognize signs, names, titles of books, and other familiar print. Generally, this stage of reading development lasts until the middle of first grade (Walker, 2005).

It is during the emergent stage of literacy development that children begin to master the concepts of print discussed above, along with phonemic awareness and the alphabetic principle. These skills are basic components of reading development in English and all other alphabetic languages. Once children understand these skills and concepts in their primary language, the knowledge can be transferred to English (Cummins, 1981). Krashen (1981) takes it a step further when he states that language acquisition in a primary language first can "actually facilitate English acquisition by providing a richer experiential base and context for acquiring this new language inside and outside the classroom" (p. 86). Not only does this support the use of strong English language development (ELD) strategies, but it also lends support to the implementation of bilingual education in the first years of schooling all ELLs, regardless of their age or grade level when entering school.

So what are the important skills and concepts that form the basis of emergent and early literacy assessment and instruction for ELLs? While it should be noted that all students require ongoing and overlapping assessment and instruction within each of the four cueing systems, this chapter specifically focuses on the concepts of print, phonemic awareness, and the alphabetic principle that rest within the construct of the graphophonic cueing system. Prior and subsequent chapters address the important skills and concepts embedded within the pragmatic, semantic, and syntactic cueing systems. This distinction is necessary to clarify the need for an assessment and instructional program that equally values each of the cueing systems.

DEFICIT THINKING:
Ways of thinking that are related to the belief that particular cultural, linguistic, or ethnic groups are genetically or culturally inferior, resulting in academic deficits. These beliefs have been around for several decades but became most prominent in the 1960s. Deficit thinking often results in qualitatively different instruction for students from underrepresented populations within the school system (Nieto, 2004).

CONCEPTS OF PRINT

Much of Marie Clay's work has been done in the area of emergent literacy, with a specific focus on the concepts of print. Clay (1993, 2002) suggests that one of the primary ways to assess students is through the systematic observation of emerging literacy behaviors. Clay is quite frank when she states that "we should abandon the (reading/writing) readiness concept. All children are ready to learn more than they already know" (p. 10). She has found that all children can learn and are ready and willing to learn when they arrive at school, regardless of their level of background knowledge, literacy development, or English language development. This is an important statement because it moves educators away from deficit thinking in regard to educating ELLs. **Deficit thinking** has been defined as the assumption that "some children, because of genetic, cultural, or experiential differences, are inferior to other children, that is, they have a deficit" (Nieto, 2004, p. 3). By observing ELLs—and all children, for that matter—through a clear lens, teachers are more able to see the strengths children bring with them to school. They can also see that all children can learn, and that those from linguistically diverse backgrounds bring with them a wealth of cultural and linguistic strengths.

Assessing the Concepts of Print

Building on these ideas, Marie Clay (1993) developed an excellent tool for observing and recording emergent and early literacy behaviors called *The Observation Survey* (1993, 2002). Referred to in a previous chapter as a standardized form of assessment, this tool can be used as it was intended—as a means of observing behaviors. *The Observation Survey* contains the following components: (a) Concepts About Print (CAP) assessment, (b) a letter identification task, (c) a writing vocabulary task, (d) a hearing and recording sounds in words task, (e) a sight word reading task, and (f) a running record assessment to determine the child's independent, instructional, and frustration reading levels. It is quite comprehensive and covers the alphabetic principle and the concepts of print in both English and Spanish.

In order to assess a student's understanding of the concepts of print, a teacher can easily use any picture book available on the classroom shelf and ask questions to determine the student's understanding of the concepts of print. Table 6.1 shows an example of a teacher-made CAP assessment developed for use with any picture book.

Teachers use observtion as a tool to assess a student's understanding of the concepts of print while engaged in a literacy lesson.

TABLE 6.1   Teacher-Made CAP Assessment: Concepts of Print Checklist

Concepts of Print	Date	Anecdotal Comments
Holds a book appropriately when reading		
Points to the front of the book		
Locates the first page of the book		
Knows that pictures are connected to the meaning of the text		
Reads left to right throughout book		
1:1 letter/sound match		
Tracks print in a 1:1 word match		
Identifies one complete sentence		
Identifies one word		
Points to the first and last words on a page		
Identifies one letter		
Identifies the first and last letters in a word		
Demonstrates that reading makes sense		
Points to the title of the book		
Knows what an author is		
Comments		

(Adapted from Clay, 1993; Johnston, 1997)

By asking questions specific to the CAP, the teacher can develop a solid picture of the student's abilities within a short time as he or she is engaged in reading an authentic text. The teacher-made CAP assessment is especially student-friendly because it can be used with books written in many languages, therefore eliminating some possible language confusions. In this way, the assessment becomes embedded within the instruction, leading to a more enjoyable experience for the teacher and the student.

PHONEMIC AWARENESS

In the past twenty years, phonemic awareness has become a much used and much debated topic in the field of literacy. In fact, it is also one of the most misunderstood concepts as well. Much of the debate is over whether it is necessary to teach phonemic awareness prior to teaching phonics and reading strategies. When reviewing the research, the findings are rather mixed (Adams, 1991; Goodman, 1986). While I will not attempt to resolve this debate, I will discuss a point that many researchers will agree on: Reading strategy instruction along with simultaneous phonics and phonemic awareness instruction embedded within the context of a meaningful and literature-rich environment provides students with powerful instruction. It is this premise that will provide the foundation for this chapter. The most important piece to consider is that ELLs whose native language is based on an alphabetic system will more easily develop or transfer phonemic awareness abilities to English than those students whose primary language is based on a logographic symbol system such as Chinese. Therefore, the time spent on these skills will vary depending on the linguistic background and level of primary language abilities of each individual ELL.

To begin the discussion on phonemic awareness, it is important to define the term. *Phonemic awareness* is "the ability to hear all of the differences in sounds and words in speech" (Fields & Spangler, 2000, p. 128). The important aspect to note is that it is solely related to the sounds heard in speech, not on their graphic representations (letters). When engaging in phonemic awareness activities and assessments, children are often playing with language through the use of songs, rhymes, and read-alouds. For example, a teacher may teach the children to sing the song, *Twinkle, Twinkle, Little Star* from memory.

> Twinkle, twinkle little <u>star,</u>
> How I wonder what you <u>are.</u>
> Up above the world so <u>high,</u>
> Like a diamond in the <u>sky.</u>
> Twinkle, twinkle little star,
> How I wonder what you are!

After learning to sing the song, the teacher will ask questions about the rhyming word pairs in the song (<u>star</u> and <u>are</u>; <u>high</u> and <u>sky</u>). By drawing the students' attention to the rhyming words, the students will begin to discriminate between sounds as well as note their similarities. Keep in mind this activity is done orally so that the letter-sound piece has yet to be presented. Once the graphic representation of the sounds has been presented, the teacher has moved into phonics instruction.

Assessing Phonemic Awareness

Phonemic awareness can be assessed both formally and informally using a variety of assessment tools. We'll begin by addressing the formal assessments before moving into a discussion of the more "classroom-friendly" assessments.

The Test of Phonological Awareness The *Test of Phonological Awareness* or *TOPA* (Torgesen & Bryant, 1994) is a standardized, norm-referenced test that assesses a student's ability to distinguish beginning and ending sounds of words. The words are read aloud and the students are asked to state whether they hear a similar or different sound. It is geared for kindergarten and first-grade students, although it can also be used for students who are in the early stages of acquiring English.

Yopp-Singer Test of Phoneme Segmentation Another assessment that may be used is the *Yopp-Singer Test of Phoneme Segmentation* (Yopp, 1995). This assessment is quick and easy to administer but must be done on an individual basis. Here the student is read a series of 22 one-syllable words. The administrator reads the list one word at a time and asks the student to separate the word into its individual sounds. For example, if the teacher reads the word *cat*, the student must say /c//ă//t/ to receive a point. It is suggested that this be used selectively with only those students who appear to be having difficulty hearing and distinguishing sounds within words. The results are not normed or standardized but instead are to be used to calculate the growth a student makes across time. Because of the simplicity of this assessment, teachers can develop their own versions of this assessment for use as pre- and posttest measures.

Elkonin Boxes Building upon the skills of phoneme segmentation presented in the Yopp-Singer assessment, Elkonin boxes (Elkonin, 1973) can be both a useful assessment and instructional tool. For early-stage ELLs this tool can be particularly useful for developing English vocabulary while also developing the ability to segment words into their individual phonemes. Teachers can purchase picture cards, cut out pictures from magazines or old calendars, or use clip art from the computer to create their own picture cards. The student will then be given the stack of picture cards, a bag of plastic chips or pennies, and an Elkonin box template such as the one found in Figure 6.1.

For each picture, the child will orally name the picture, slowly say the word again listening for the individual sounds of the phonemes, and slide a penny into a box for each sound heard. Initially, this activity should be modeled by the teacher until the student feels comfortable with the process of stretching or "rubber banding" the words (Calkins, 1986). Once the student is ready to try it out, it would be best if the ELL worked in collaboration with a classmate in order to allow him or her to discuss the pic-

Elkonin Box with 5 sound spaces

😃	😃	😃	😃	😃

Picture Cards

Word: tiger

(Extra pennies)

FIGURE 6.1   Elkonin Box Assessment Tool
Adapted from Elkonin, 1973.

tures and sounds as the activity is completed. Once the ELL is familiar with how to use the Elkonin box, the teacher can then observe the student engaging in the activity and note his or her progress made across time. This activity can also help the teacher to determine if further instruction is needed in phoneme segmentation. Elkonin boxes are excellent assessment tools because they appear to be more of a game to students, thus decreasing their level of anxiety and hopefully increasing their level of success.

Teacher-Made Rhyming Assessments   Because the components of phonemic awareness are fairly simple, the use of teacher-made assessments seems prudent. Teachers can create lists of rhyming words and nonrhyming words and ask the students to state whether they rhyme. An example of a teacher-created rhyming-words phonemic awareness assessment can be found in Table 6.2.

TABLE 6.2   Rhyming Words Phonemic Awareness Teacher-Made Assessment

Teacher Prompt: You are going to listen to several word pairs. I want you to tell me if they rhyme. For example, do the words *hat* and *sat* rhyme? Say "yes" if they rhyme and "no" if they do not rhyme. OK, let's try another example. Do the words *door* and *dot* rhyme?

Word Pairs	*Response (C = Correct)*	*Pretest Date*	*Posttest Date*
sun/fun			
hot/boat			
right/fight			
sky/fly			
door/floor			
hurt/shirt			
house/grass			

As you can see from the word pairs presented in Table 6.2, teachers can easily create these word lists based on the background knowledge and level of English language development of their students. In order to make this task more manageable for second language learners, it might be helpful to use picture cards along with the oral naming of the words so that they are also presented with a meaningful representation of the word. By adding the visual connection, this assessment can also have instructional value. The assessment results can then be tallied, dated, and placed in the students' portfolios to chart their progress across time.

The Lindamood Auditory Conceptualization Test   An additional phonemic awareness assessment that can used with older, more experienced ELLs is the *Lindamood Auditory Conceptualization Test (LAC;* Lindamood & Lindamood, 1979). The LAC is divided into three main sections: (a) identification of phonemes, (b) blending and segmenting phonemes, and (c) making phoneme substitutions. The test begins with easier tasks and becomes progressively more difficult. This assessment is administered on a one-to-one basis and generally takes 15 to 20 minutes from start to finish. Here the teacher says a word such as *dog* and asks the student to represent the number of sounds within the word using colored blocks, with each color of block representing a different sound. After spending as much time as needed explaining and practicing the process, the student continues until completing each of the tasks. Often the most difficult part of this assessment is learning how to complete the task using the blocks. Time spent practicing the activity is time well spent. For those students who are more visual and kinesthetic learners, this may prove to be the best form of assessment for them. This assessment is also standardized and normed for various age levels, thus increasing its level of validity and reliability.

In summary, it is important to keep in mind that early-stage ELLs may require multiple exposures to a skill or concept before they are able to master it. Because they are also in the initial stages of English acquisition (Tompkins, 2006), they therefore may need to practice each of the assessments many times prior to the actual testing session. By doing this, the students will feel more at ease and will be more likely to provide an accurate indication of their true abilities.

THE ALPHABETIC PRINCIPLE

Children begin to develop the concepts of print, phonemic awareness, and knowledge of the alphabetic principle when they are exposed to books, songs, and rhymes prior to entering school. Morrow (2001) has suggested that children can learn the alphabetic principle in school through engagement in the type of authentic literacy activities modeled by parents at home. Creating learning centers full of game-like activities will motivate children to play with language, and in turn, learn valuable language skills and concepts. Teaching children to count the number of sounds and syllables in words as they listen to stories helps them to attend to sounds and syllables as they learn to read

Students often experiment with written language in a variety of settings. Here a student responds to a book by drawing the main characters and writing their names.

(Yopp & Troyer, 1992). This leads them into reading as a natural next step in the process of acquiring language.

Assessing Knowledge of the Alphabetic Principle

Understanding the alphabetic principle requires a student to make a connection between the sounds heard in the spoken word and then to transfer this knowledge to the printed word. To better understand a student's ability to make this transfer, teachers need to find assessments to determine the student's baseline knowledge level and continue to assess the student as he or she progresses through the school year. These assessments can be more formal or may take place during the course of instruction. The next section will detail both types of assessment.

The Letter-Naming Task   As previously mentioned, *The Observation Survey* (Clay, 1993, 2002) contains a letter-naming task. This assessment is relatively quick to administer and score. Here the students are presented with a page containing the 26 letters of the uppercase alphabet. The letters are randomly placed on the page so the teacher is sure that the student can actually recognize and name the letter when it is seen out of order. The student is then asked to provide the letter's sound, or if unable to do so, to provide a word that begins with the letter. Incorrect responses are noted on the score sheet.

Next, the student is asked to identify the lowercase letters of the alphabet. Again, the lowercase letters are in random order on the testing sheet. Additionally, the typewritten letters "a" and "g" are on the sheet as well. The purpose is to ensure that the student is able to recognize different forms of the same letters. Together the scores for the upper- and lowercase letter naming and sound identification tasks are tallied, providing the teacher with a numeric score for the student. Norms are provided for those students in grades 1 and 2. *The Observation Survey* is also available in a Spanish language version.

The Ekwall-Shanker Reading Inventory   The *Ekwall-Shanker Reading Inventory,* 4th edition (Ekwall & Shanker, 2000) consists of ten subtests covering the following skills and concepts: (1) The Basic Sight Words and Phrases Test, (2) The Letter Knowledge Test, (3) The Phonics Test, (4) The Structural Analysis Test, (5) The Knowledge of Contractions Test, (6) The El Paso Phonics Survey, (7) The San Diego Quick, (8) graded reading passages portion, (9) The Reading Interests Survey, and (10) The Emergent Literacy Test. This is one of the most comprehensive reading inventories on the market, covering the preprimer level up through grade 9. Depending on the student's level of alphabetic knowledge, teachers need to be very selective when using this assessment, choosing those pieces that best meet the needs of their individual ELLs and English-only students. Because it has four equivalent forms, it can be used as a pre- and posttest measure. Keep in mind that this is very comprehensive, which also means it is quite time-consuming. In an attempt to save time and embed assessment within classroom instruction, the next section will describe more teacher-friendly assessments.

Teacher-Friendly Assessments Many teachers have a designated silent reading time period each day. As a modification on the silent reading period, it can be beneficial to allow students to read aloud with a partner. During this time period the teacher can then rotate around from group to group observing and taking notes on the students' reading behaviors. It would also be a time to note the students' word attack skills and ability to decode words. Teachers can then quickly assess each student's knowledge of the alphabetic principle and address those areas that need further development during a small group lesson.

GUIDED READING: *"A context in which a teacher supports each reader's development of effective strategies for processing novel texts at increasingly challenging levels of difficulty" (Fountas & Pinnell, 1996, p. 2). Teachers work with small flexible groups of readers needing instruction on similar reading strategies. The instruction is focused, text-based, and within the readers' Zone of Proximal Development.*

Guided reading is a time when a teacher can prepare a minilesson on a phonics or word recognition strategy that would benefit the students in the group. **Guided reading** (Clay, 1993, 2002; Fountas & Pinnell, 1996) is a teaching model used by both primary and intermediate level teachers. First developed by Marie Clay as a part of the Reading Recovery Intervention Program, it soon spread to the mainstream classroom. Guided reading is an interaction between the teacher and a small group of students who have been placed together because of a similar need. Within guided reading, the teacher introduces the students to a book that contains an example of the concept to be taught in a minilesson. For example, if the students are all experiencing difficulties with decoding compound words, they would be grouped together for their instruction. It should be noted that the groups are flexible, and students frequently move from group to group. The use of guided reading groups promotes relevant instruction while also allowing the teacher to make observations and assessments on a regular basis. Teachers can also take running records during these sessions and note the types and qualities of miscues made when reading. These observations are recorded and placed in the students' portfolios to document progress. A sample teacher-made recording sheet can be found in Table 6.3.

Additionally, teachers can prepare their own letter-naming assessments with pictures and/or letter tiles for use during the guided reading lesson. For example, the students may be working on onsets and rimes using letter tiles. The teacher would instruct them to make the word *dog* using the tiles and check their understanding. Next she would ask them to take the word *dog* and turn it into the word *hog*, thus manipulating the initial sound or *onset* of the word. If the teacher wanted to work on the ending portion (medial vowel and ending letter) or *rime* of the word, she might ask the students to take the word *bat* and turn it into the word *big*, all the while informally assessing the students' knowledge of the alphabetic principle.

Many simple teaching techniques such as the ones previously mentioned can be used as assessments that have been embedded within the context of instruction. The use of such assessments, especially for ELLs, helps them to feel comfortable and willing to take risks when learning. This is extremely important to their overall success in school.

TABLE 6.3   Early Literacy Assessment Portfolio Sheet

Child's Name: _____ Grade: _____

Date	Assessment Administered	Child's Strengths/ Areas of Need	Instructional Recommendations
	<u>Concepts of Print:</u> An assessment that shows what a child knows about letters, sounds, words, directionality, picture cues, tracking, and punctuation.		
	<u>Observation Survey:</u> **Letter Identification:** A task used to determine if a child can name the upper- and lowercase letters of the alphabet and also distinguish the sound made by each letter.		
	Hearing Sounds in Words: A task that requires the child to record a dictated sentence. The product is scored by counting the phonemes that are represented using letters.		
	Word Reading: A sight word reading assessment consisting of 15 high-frequency words. The child is scored for reading accuracy.		
	Writing Vocabulary: An observational writing task in which a child is given 10 minutes to write down all of the words in his or her writing vocabulary. It is scored for accuracy of spelling.		

(Continued)

TABLE 6.3   *(Continued)*

Date	Assessment Administered	Child's Strengths/ Areas of Need	Instructional Recommendations
	Running Record: A systematic reading miscue assessment based on a 100-word passage from a leveled text. It is used to determine a child's use of reading strategies, the type and quality of miscues made when reading orally, and the correct level of text for independent and instructional reading.		
	Interest Inventory: An informal measure of a child's reading, writing, and personal interests. The results are used to help a teacher select high-interest texts and instructional materials and strategies.		
	Writing Sample: A writing sample, of varying genres, collected at various intervals throughout the ten-week tutoring period. The samples are scored using a rubric based on the six traits of writing as well as through writing conferences and self-reflection.		
	Teacher-Made Rhyming Assessment: An oral assessment that measures the ability to discriminate between sounds and identify rhyming words.		

Strategies Promoting Development of the Concepts of Print, Phonemic Awareness, and the Alphabetic Principle

This section of the chapter provides a list of excellent teaching strategies that can also be used as informal assessments of the alphabetic principle. Use of these strategies will engage all students in meaningful instruction.

- Wide reading in a variety of genres
- Daily read-alouds, shared reading, and interactive reading
- Guided reading two to three times per week at all grade levels
- Language Experience Approach
- Rubber-banding of words
- Open and closed word sorts
- Onsets and rimes card games
- Word play through the use of rhymes, alliteration, and songs
- Alphabet concentration
- Picture card identification games
- Word walls
- Writing across the content areas
- Phonetic spelling instruction

REVISITING THE *CHAPTER ANTICIPATION GUIDE*

Spend a few minutes reviewing the statements presented in the Chapter Anticipation Guide at the beginning of the chapter. Compare your notes with those **highlighted**.

End-of-the-Chapter Anticipation Guide

Agree	Disagree	Statement
✗		ELLs can transfer skills and concepts learned in their primary language into English. *True—Primary language skills may also serve to facilitate English acquisition for students both inside and outside of the classroom. By sharing this information with ELLs, they will also see how their primary language is valued, which in turn enhances their ability to learn English and other new languages.*

Agree	Disagree	Statement
	✗	Marie Clay's *Observation Survey* was intended to be used as a readiness assessment for teachers. *False—Marie Clay is against readiness testing for children and created her assessment as an observational tool for teachers. It was her hope that it would take the place of some of the readiness tests in place in schools.*
	✗	*Phonics* and *phonemic awareness* are essentially interchangeable terms. *False—Phonics and phonemic awareness are two different yet related concepts. Phonics deals with sound-symbol relationships while phonemic awareness is solely related to the sounds made when speaking. The English language has 44 phonemes and only 26 letters.*
✗		The use of daily read-alouds promotes the development of emergent and early reading skills and concepts for ELLs of all ages. *True—Through the use of read-alouds of all levels and genres, teachers can expose children to the syntactic, semantic, and phonetic components of the English language. If big books are used, teachers can also show the graphophonic features of the language while reading. It is a meaningful, authentic way to provide English language instruction as well as literacy concepts and modeling of fluent reading. It's an all-around win–win situation for everyone!*
	✗	ELLs must have mastered the concepts of print and the alphabetic principle and have demonstrated a high degree of phonemic awareness prior to being exposed to authentic texts and other reading material. *False—It is a misconception that ELLs and early and emergent readers cannot interact with real texts until they have mastered all of their letters and sounds. This is especially true when you consider that many English words are not purely phonetic and therefore cannot be read solely using phonics. By waiting to introduce real books, the ELLs will be at a disadvantage from their peers. They will not be able to learn rich vocabulary, story structure, and the syntactic features of the English language.*

ASSESSMENT *TOOLKIT*

Concepts of Print

- Picture books for all ages, interest levels, and reading levels.
- Teacher-made CAP assessment form.
- *The Observation Survey* (Clay, 2002) with copies of each of the assessments.
- Blank paper and pencils.
- Big books and sticky notes.
- Clipboard and paper to jot down observations.

ASSESSMENT *TOOLKIT*

Phonemic Awareness

- Picture cards (cut from magazines, old calendars, or or premade).
- Laminated Elkonin boxes with 2, 3, 4, 5, and 6 squares.
- Bags of pennies or chips.
- Copies of rhyming poems, songs, and chants.
- Copies of the *Yopp-Singer Phoneme Awareness Test*.
- Copies of the teacher-made rhyming word assessment.

ASSESSMENT *TOOLKIT*

The Alphabetic Principle

- Guided reading books containing varying word patterns.
- Blank running record sheets.
- Letter-naming assessment sheets.
- Books of varying genres and textual structures.
- Letter tiles.
- Picture cards/word cards.

CHAPTER SEVEN

Assessment and Development of Word Identification, Comprehension, and Reading Fluency

TEACHER *VIGNETTE*

Suzanne is a fifth-grade teacher in an urban elementary school in Southern California. During a class discussion in a literacy assessment course, she raised her hand in response to a question regarding fluency assessment and instruction of ELLs and English-only students. Suzanne spoke with a great deal of passion as she recounted the following scenario:

"I am getting so upset about doing fluency tests in my fifth-grade classroom. The majority of my students are English language learners who are working hard to learn to read, write, and speak in English. They are all ready under a great deal of pressure to succeed in school and to 'fit in' to the peer culture on campus without the need for extra pressure to be put on them to read faster. I am required to give a fluency test each quarter that goes on their report card and makes up a majority of their grade. Because of the pressures put on them to read faster and faster on these tests, many of the students are starting to miss school during testing time due to a variety of physical ailments. Some of my students go home sick on those days and I've even had a few students wet their pants. Keep in mind, I teach fifth grade."

When asked how she is dealing with the pressure of these fluency tests, Suzanne said that she tells her students to read the passages and skip over the words they don't know. "In fact, it's the only time I tell my students to read that fast and not to worry about the meaning of the words they are reading. That way, they feel less pressure to remember what they've read but they can also read faster and get a better grade."

While Suzanne has found a way to adapt to some of the pressures of fluency assessment for her students, she has lingering concerns about the misuse of the term fluency for these tests. In reality, this type of test is really measuring reading rate. What is the definition of fluency and how do these tests impact the students' view of the purpose of reading? How does this impact an ELL as he or she begins to read in English?

Suzanne, 2006

The vignette presented above relates a story that is common among teachers in today's schools. There is a great deal of confusion as to the meaning of the term *fluency* as well as the most effective and meaningful ways of assessing a learner's level of reading fluency. Teachers are often pressured to assess ELLs using methods that are stressful and prove to be an invalid measure of reading fluency. Additionally, ELLs may be assessed in their second language while the level of reading fluency in their native language is neglected. By ignoring their native reading abilities, many ELLs are incor-

Teaching modeling is an essential component in the development of fluent readers.

rectly viewed as poor readers, leaving them with a lifelong label that is difficult to overcome. It is essential for classroom teachers to understand the intricacies of reading fluency in order to correctly assess and instruct ELLs. The next section details the most current research on fluency, leading to a deeper understanding of the complex construct of reading fluency.

An Expanded Definition of Reading Fluency

Fluency is a concept that has been fundamentally linked to reading ability for centuries, although the exact definition of what constitutes fluent reading has been quite varied. From 1600 to 1850, the ability to sign one's name was often seen as a measure of reading fluency. It was not until after 1850 that more precise methods of determining literacy levels—and in turn, reading fluency levels—were developed (Kaestle, Damon-Moore, Stedman, Tinsley, & Trollinger, 1991). In more recent decades, fluency has been seen as the ability to read with speed, accuracy, and expression (National

Reading Panel, 2000; Samuels, 2002). This definition refers to a reader's ability to decode print orally with little or no word recognition difficulties, and in a manner that is representative of the natural flow of language. Nowhere in this definition will you find reference to the meaning or comprehension of the words being recited.

Presently, a more distinctive description of the nature of fluency has been developed that adds the needed comprehension component.

> *Reading fluency* refers to the efficient, effective word-recognition skills that permit a reader to construct the meaning of a text. Fluency is manifested in accurate, rapid, expressive oral reading and is applied during, and makes possible, silent *reading comprehension.* (Pikulski & Chard, 2005, p. 510)

Within the definition of reading fluency proposed by Pikulski and Chard (2005), it should be noted that fluency no longer just refers to the area of oral reading but adds a comprehension piece that lends itself to silent reading comprehension as well. While this may seem like a minor revision of past descriptions of fluency, it is actually of great importance to the teaching of reading. The authors go on to discuss "surface" versus "deep" fluency levels, implying the necessity of using the deep fluency model within a developmental framework of teaching reading. Within this framework, fluency is seen "as part of a development process of building decoding skills that will form a bridge to reading comprehension and that will have a reciprocal, causal relationship with reading comprehension" (Pikulski & Chard, 2005, p. 511). In other words, without word accuracy, speed, expression, and comprehension, fluent reading has not taken place (see Figure 7.1).

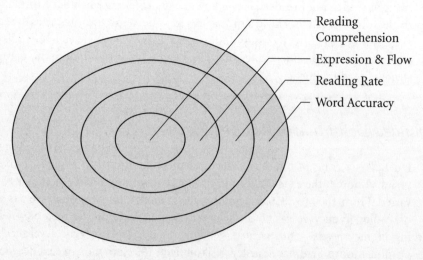

Reading Comprehension

Expression & Flow

Reading Rate

Word Accuracy

FIGURE 7.1   Model of Reading Fluency

Adopting the expanded definition of reading fluency clarifies the type of assessments, and subsequently, instruction that would benefit ELLs. Fluency assessments should include a balance of word recognition tasks, measures of flow and expression, and a comprehension check of the content of the text being read. Without each of these components, a true picture of the learner's strengths and needs is unlikely to emerge. To support the development of such a balanced fluency assessment system, the next section will detail the most meaningful fluency assessments that can be utilized with ELLs.

Running Records and Retellings

Based on the expanded fluency definition presented above, it becomes important to first determine the learner's level of fluency when reading a text in his or her primary language. One of the fastest and most inexpensive methods of assessing primary language reading fluency is to obtain a piece of text from the learner's primary language that is approximately 100 words in length. Using the text, the teacher can have the student read the text aloud while taking a **running record** on a separate sheet of paper.

RUNNING RECORD:
A detailed description of the reading behaviors exhibited as a learner reads a text aloud. It is a written record of the learner's miscues, repetitions, self-corrections, omissions, insertions, substitutions, and accurate pronunciations of words in a passage. A running record should be taken of three different texts or passages in order to obtain an accurate account of the learner's strengths and needs. (Clay, 1993, 2002)

It may be necessary to have a native speaker available during the assessment to provide insights into the nuances of the specific language of the learner and clarify any misconceptions that may occur. A running record should be done three times using three different texts/genres/topics to ensure the accuracy of the findings. The piece of text utilized can be reprinted on a separate piece of paper, allowing the teacher to quickly record the learner's responses on the text, or the teacher can use a standard running record sheet (see Appendix A).

Prior to collecting a running record, the teacher should spend a few minutes assessing the learner's background knowledge of the topic(s) addressed in the passage. If the learner's knowledge base is minimal, it would be prudent to select a different passage. The reason this is important is that the ELL may seem to be a disfluent reader when, in reality, he or she may only be unfamiliar with the content of the passage. Therefore, the running record may provide the teacher with an inaccurate representation of the learner's true fluency level. Because of this, it would be wise to provide the student with an expository text, a narrative text, and a third textual genre as well. Reutzel and Cooter (2003) also suggest allowing the learner to read through the passages one or two times prior to taking a running record to simulate an authentic reading situation as much as possible.

After recording the learner's responses on the running record sheet, calculate the number of "substantial miscues" made when reading. *Substantial miscues* refers to those miscues that have changed the meaning of the text. If the miscues are substan-

FIGURE 7.2   Calculating Accuracy Levels for a Running Record

Divide the **number of words read correctly** and the **nonsubstantial miscues** by the **number of words in the passage** to figure out the percentage of words read accurately.

$$\frac{\text{\# words read correctly} + \text{nonsubstantial miscues}}{\text{\# words in the passage (running words)}} = \text{Accuracy Percentage}$$

tial, it shows that the reader is not reading for meaning at that point in time. Based on these miscues, accuracy percentages can be calculated using the formula in Figure 7.2.

Once you have calculated the accuracy percentages, use the information in Table 7.1 to determine the reader's appropriate reading level. Generally, these percentages (see Table 7.1) are considered when determining an independent reading level, an instructional reading level, and the level of reading frustration (Clay, 1972, 1985, 1997; Gunning, 2002).

After completing the running record, have the student do an oral retelling of the passage as you record, verbatim, what is said. The retelling provides the teacher with a comprehension check of the material being read. Retellings have been found to be one of the most time-efficient and sound methods of assessing reading comprehension (Gambrell, Pfeiffer, & Wilson, 1985; Hoyt, 1998; Morrow, 1985). While many teachers prefer to ask a series of questions after a learner reads a text selection, a retelling provides a more effective means of measuring progress over time (Reutzel & Cooter, 2003). If the retelling is omitted, an essential element of the fluency assessment has also been

TABLE 7.1   Reading Level Percentages

Reading Levels	Oral Reading Accuracy Percentages (of Significant Miscues)	Comprehension Percentages (Using Questions)	Comprehension Percentages (Using Retelling Sheet)
Independent Reading Level	95–100%	90–100%	90–100%
Instructional Reading Level	90–94%	75–89%	75–89%
Frustration Reading Level	≤ 89%	≥ 74%	≥ 74%

(Based on Clay, 1991; Gunning, 2002)

left out. Because the running record is being done using a primary language text, the retelling should also be done in the learner's primary language. It may be necessary to tape record the retelling and have it transcribed by a native speaker to ensure its accuracy. For short passages, a modified version of the analysis sheet can be used.

Figure 7.3 shows a narrative retelling analysis sheet that has been developed as a means to score the retelling of a narrative text.

FIGURE 7.3   **Narrative Story Retelling Analysis Sheet**

Narrative Story Retelling Assessment

Child's Name: _____ Age: ___9___

Name of Story: _____

Date: _____

How Story Was Read: _____ Orally _____ Silently _____ **Read to Student**
(check one)

Directions: Score each story element based on the child's retelling. Point values are included next to each element. The student will receive more points if the student directly states the answer within his or her retelling without being prompted.

P = Prompted Response   UP = Unprompted Response

   A. **Names main character** [2 points unprompted (UP); 1 point prompted (P)]:

   B. **Names other important characters** [2 points UP; 1 point P] :

   C. **Names setting** [2 points UP; 1 point P] :

   D. **Includes important events in the story** (All = 4 UP, Most = 3 UP, Few = 2 UP; 1 = P):

   E. **Problem is stated** [2 points UP; 1 point P] :

   F. **Resolution is stated** [2 points UP; 1 point P] :

   G. **Story is told in sequence** (Yes = 3 UP, Partially = 2 UP; 1 point P]

   H. **Concludes story** [2 points UP; 1 point P] :

   I.   **States story theme or moral** [1 point P]

Highest Score Possible: 20   **Child's Score:** _____

Comments:

(Brantley, 2004)

In the narrative story retelling analysis, the teacher first parses the story that is going to be retold into the following categories: (1) setting, (2) main characters, (3) story problem, (4) series of events (3 to 8 main events in order of occurrence in the story), (5) problem resolution, and (6) moral or theme of the story. These can be modified to fit the particular story being retold. An example of a parsed story is provided in Figure 7.4. It shows the components of a common story that can be used to assess a stu-

FIGURE 7.4   Parsed Story: *The Magic Flute* by Amy Cackett (n.d.)

Title: <u>The Magic Flute</u> Author: Amy F. Cackett

Main Character: Prince Boldheart

Other Characters:, Princess Villette, the Ogre, the old man named Encourage.

Setting: In a castle in the middle of the country surrounded by a forest.

Main Story Events (in order):

1. There was place where everyone was should have been happy but they were not because of the ogre that lived in the castle protected by a dragon.

2. The ogre would come out of the castle and play his flute. The flute would turn people to stone so they couldn't move while the music played.

3. Prince Boldheart was afraid the ogre would take his "soon to be wife" Princess Villette so he watched out for the princess.

4. One day when he was out hunting, the Prince heard the music and became frozen. The ogre had taken his Princess.

5. A man named Encourage gave the Prince a drink to make him brave.

6. The Prince met and fought the dragon after realizing that he could do it because he had taken the potion.

7. He thought brave thoughts as he moved through the forest and conquered all of the obstacles.

8. The castle came crashing down and he rescued the Princess and all the others that had been taken away.

9. The Prince married the Princess and lived happily ever after.

Moral of the Story: You can behave bravely if you believe in yourself. You can do anything you put your mind to it.

FIGURE 7.5   Arturo's Retelling

The story was about a Prince who wanted to marry a princess but she got taken away by a monster. The monster lived in a castle and played the flute a lot so he could steal people and turn them into rocks. The Princess's mom and dad died and she wanted to get married. She lived in a palace. The prince didn't protect her and she got stolen and turned to stone. Then he drank some water and got the princess and everyone else. They got married.

dent's ability to retell a story with sufficient detail. It is important to parse the story prior to asking the student to retell it so that the teacher is aware of the appropriate story sequence and number of events within a story.

Figure 7.5 shows a copy of an oral retelling of the story given by an ELL named Arturo. Arturo is a fourth-grade student who has been in the United States for approximately three years. He attends an English immersion program at his local school site and has done so since arriving in the United States. Arturo read the story in his native language of Spanish and retold it in Spanish as well. His retelling has been translated into English for this text.

After completing the retelling, Arturo's teacher transferred his responses to the story retelling analysis sheet (see Figure 7.6).

As you can see from his scores, Arturo was able to name the main characters from the story and recall some of the details, but he was unable to retell the story in the proper sequence of events. He was able to state the story problem and resolution, but was unsure of where the story took place. From his retelling, his teacher determined that Arturo was able to provide the overall gist of the story, although he did require some prompting. He named the main character and supporting characters and was able to retell some of the story events in sequence. While he understood the problem in the story, he was unable to infer the main theme or moral of the story. Arturo had a fairly well-developed sense of story that his teacher had been previously unaware of. His teacher was able to use this information to provide Arturo with relevant instruction and then reassess at varying intervals to chart his progress. By incorporating story retellings into the classroom as an assessment and an instructional strategy, teachers have a relatively quick and valuable tool for assessing comprehension within the context of instruction.

Additionally, it can be helpful to determine the learner's reading rate as well by timing the student as he or she reads through the 100- to 200-word passage. Such oral reading data can be used to "get a sense of a student's global reading ability and monitor the progress of that student over time" (Wiley & Deno, 2005, p. 212). While this information is useful, it should be noted that it is most helpful to chart the student's

FIGURE 7.6   **Arturo's Narrative Story Retelling Analysis Sheet**

Narrative Story Retelling Assessment

Child's Name: **Arturo**   Age: _____9_____

Name of Story: **The Magic Flute**

Date: **11/23**

How Story Was Read: __×__ Orally _____ Silently _____ Read to Student
(check one)

Directions: Score each story element based on the child's retelling. Point values are included next to each element. The student will receive more points if the student directly states the answer within his or her retelling without being prompted.

P = Prompted Response UP = Unprompted Response

  I. Names main character [2 points unprompted (UP); 1 point prompted (P)]: 2

  J. Names other important characters [2 points UP; 1 point P] : 1

  K. Names setting [2 points UP; 1 point P] : 1

  L. Includes important events in the story (All = 4 UP, Most = 3 UP, Few = 2 UP; 1 = P): 2

  M. Problem is stated [2 points UP; 1 point P] : 2

  N. Resolution is stated [2 points UP; 1 point P] : 1

  O. Story is told in sequence (Yes = 3 UP, Partially = 2 UP; 1 point P] : 1

  P. Concludes story [2 points UP; 1 point P] : 1

  I. States story theme or moral [1 point P] : 0

Highest Score Possible: 20   Child's Score: _____11_____

Comments: Arturo was able to provide the overall gist of the story, although it did require some prompting. He named the main character and supporting characters and was able to retell some of the story events in sequence. While he understood the problem in the story, he was unable to infer the main theme or moral of the story.

(Brantley, 2004)

TABLE 7.2   Sample Fluency Recording Sheet

Name: _____   Grade Level: _____

Date	New (N) or Familiar (F) Text	Title and Genre of Text	Words per Minute

individual progress over time rather than use the data as a means of comparison between students. It is also important to remember that this is just one reading measure among many that will be used to develop a profile of the student's abilities.

To reduce the level of pressure being put on the student, this evaluation can be done in a subtle manner by recording the time the student started reading and marking where he or she was at the end of one minute. Teachers can then calculate the student's reading rate at a later time by counting the number of words he or she read in the one-minute time period. This data can then be kept inside of the learner's reading portfolio and tracked over time using a simple format such as the one found in Table 7.2.

Be sure to note whether the fluency test is taking place in the learner's primary language or English and whether the reading was based on a new text or a familiar text. This information puts the reading rate into the proper perspective, and you will be able to note trends across time.

Once the running record, story retelling, and reading rate have been completed in the learner's primary language, the next step is to repeat the process using appropriately leveled materials written in English. During the process of analyzing and evaluating the results, you will be able to note strengths and needs in both languages and note any similarities and differences across the two (or more) languages. This information will be useful when planning instruction.

Informal Reading Inventories (IRIs)

Informal Reading Inventories or IRIs are excellent tools for determining an ELL's level of reading proficiency in English and a second language, such as Spanish. The Flynt and Cooter (2004) IRI is available in English and Spanish and contains both narrative and expository passages. Generally, all IRIs contain multiple yet equivalent leveled passages so teachers can use them as a tool for pre- and posttesting a student. IRIs are leveled ac-

Written retellings can be used as a means of assessing a student's listening, silent, and oral comprehension levels.

cording to grade levels and are generally made to cover preprimer levels through grade 12. All IRIs contain graded word lists and/or graded sentences as a means of determining the level of passage to begin administering the assessment. Table 7.3 contains information regarding various IRIs that are presently on the market. Each has its strengths and weaknesses so it's best to find the IRI that is most suited to a particular teacher and classroom population.

When administering an IRI, it is valuable to do a complete assessment of the ELL's abilities to read and comprehend in English, and if available, in his or her primary language. A teacher will want to determine a student's oral, silent, and listening comprehension levels along with the student's ability to decode words in context and isolation. Most IRIs use the same accuracy percentages as found in Table 7.1.

This information will allow a teacher to understand all facets of a student's reading ability. Some students are uncomfortable reading aloud, so they may fare much better when reading silently. Other students comprehend at a higher level when they are able to see and hear the words as they read orally. By assessing a student's listening comprehension level, a teacher will be able to determine the appropriate level of texts to use when reading aloud. Administering an IRI can be a time-consuming process but well worth the investment because of the amount of information gleaned. Because of the

TABLE 7.3   Informal Reading Inventories

Name/Grades of Informal Reading Inventory (IRI)	Languages Available	Publisher's Information for Each IRI
Reading Inventory for the Classroom (5th ed.) (PP-9)	English and Spanish	E. Sutton Flynt & Robert Cooter (2004). Merrill/Prentice Hall
Informal Reading Inventory (6th ed.) (PP -12)	English	Paul Burns & Betty Roe (2002). Houghton Mifflin
The Stieglitz Informal Reading Inventory (3rd ed.) (PP-9)	English	Ezra L. Stieglitz (2002). Allyn and Bacon
Ekwall/Shanker Reading Inventory (4th ed.) (PP-9)	English	James Shanker & Eldon Ekwall (2000). Merrill/Prentice Hall
Bader Reading and Language Inventory (4th ed.) (K-12/adult)	English	Lois Bader (2002). Merrill/Prentice Hall
Qualitative Reading Inventory-3 (3rd ed.) (PP-12)	English	Lauren Leslie & JoAnne Caldwell (2001). Allyn and Bacon
Analytical Reading Inventory (7th ed.) (K-12)	English	Mary Lynn Woods & Alden Moe (2003). Merrill/Prentice Hall
Critical Reading Inventory (PP-12)	English	Mary DeKonty Applegate, Kathleen Benson Quinn, & Anthony J. Applegate (2004). Merrill/Prentice Hall.

time factor, a teacher may want to use an IRI as pre- and post-assessments at the beginning and end of a school year to calculate the amount of growth made by a student.

Cloze Passages

A simple strategy for assessing an ELL's vocabulary level and for determining a reading level is to provide the student with an appropriately leveled cloze passage to complete. A cloze passage is basically a fill-in-the-blank test in which every fifth or sixth word has been deleted. The student must then use context clues and surrounding vocabulary to fill in the missing word. Passages can be taken directly from textbooks when assessing content area vocabulary, or teachers can create their own cloze passages. When scoring the passage, teachers are to only accept as correct the exact word that came from the original text. Cloze passages can be extremely difficult for students and therefore are scored using a much more relaxed set of criteria. If students accurately complete the passage at the 50 percent level, it is considered to be at the appropriate level for classroom instruction. If it at or below the 40 percent range, it is at the student's frustration level and should not be used (Lenski & Nierstheimer, 2004). Either way, be very careful when using cloze passages because they tend to be much more difficult than they first appear.

Evaluating the Assessment Results

After collecting data on the ELL's ability to decode and pronounce words, read a text fluently, and comprehend it, the task of determining the most appropriate and relevant instruction begins. The next section will list several strategies that can be implemented in a small group and/or whole group classroom setting. Be selective in your use of the strategies and spend enough time teaching each strategy so that the student will reach a level of mastery. The key is to provide depth rather than attempting to expose them to all of the strategies in one school year.

Strategies to Build Word Recognition, Comprehension, and Fluency

The following list of strategies are beneficial when instructing ELLs in the areas of word recognition, reading and/or listening comprehension, and reading fluency:

- Language Experience Approach
- Guided reading
- Mini shared reading
- Collaborative reading
- Assisted reading
- Anticipation guides
- DRTA and DLTA
- K-W-L-Q
- SQ3R
- Paragraph frames
- Use of word banks and word walls
- Picture Word Inductive Model

- Wide reading, read-alouds, partner reading
- Semantic maps and graphic organizers
- Comparison grids
- Word study activities such as word sorts and Making Words
- Reader's and writer's workshop
- Use of environmental print and visual aids
- Reader's theater, plays, poetry, creative drama
- Repeated readings
- Neurological Impress Method
- Fluency Development Lesson (FDL)
- Oral and written retellings
- Reciprocal teaching
- QAR

While these strategies are but a few that are available to word identification skills, comprehension, and build fluency, they have all been found to be engaging and meaningful for students. They are also outstanding strategies to implement class-wide with all of your students.

REVISITING THE *CHAPTER ANTICIPATION GUIDE*

Spend a few minutes reviewing the statements presented in the Chapter Anticipation Guide at the beginning of the chapter. Compare your notes with those **highlighted**.

End-of-the-Chapter Anticipation Guide

Agree	Disagree	Statement
	✘	Fluency is best defined as the speed at which a reader can decode a text. *False—Fluency is made up of three equally important components: reading rate and flow, word accuracy, and comprehension. All must be present to be considered a fluent reader.*
✘		Running records provide teachers with an accurate picture of a learner's reading behaviors. *True—A running record provides a teacher with a window into the invisible processes taking place as a student decodes a text. Running records are further enhanced when a retelling component is added.*

Agree	Disagree	Statement
✗		An ELL's level of fluency should be measured in his or her primary and secondary languages to ensure accurate results. *True—In order to form an accurate picture of an ELL's strengths and needs, assessment should take place in L1 and L2. Skills developed in L1 are often transferable to L2. Why not view first language abilities as an asset!*
✗		Word recognition strategies learned in a primary language enhance word recognition abilities in a second language. *True—I just addressed this very issue in the previous box.*
	✗	Systematic phonics instruction is the most effective means of reading words at all levels of text. *Hmm . . . while this may work for some students when reading decodable texts, students often need to employ all of the cueing systems in order to read with fluency and comprehension. Readers need to use all of the tools available to them to understand a text.*

ASSESSMENT *TOOLKIT*

Word Identification, Comprehension, and Word Fluency

- Several 100- to 200-word passages at various reading levels, various languages, and in the various genres of writing.
- Clock with a second hand.
- Tape recorder and inexpensive blank tapes. Label one with the name of each student in the class and place the recorder and tapes at a table in the classroom.
- Informal Reading Inventory, put together in two binders: one for the pretest and one for the posttest (in multiple languages if possible).
- Cloze passages of varying genres and at different reading levels. They should be about 250 words in length

CHAPTER EIGHT

Assessment and Development of Written Language and Spelling

Read through each of the following statements prior to reading the chapter. Place a checkmark in either the box labeled "agree" or "disagree" depending upon whether you believe the statement to be true or false. As you read the chapter, refer back to the chart and confirm or modify your initial responses.

Initial Chapter Anticipation Guide

Agree	Disagree	Statement
		Spelling and vocabulary essentially require identical skills and therefore identical instructional techniques.
		ELLs should not receive instruction in writing until they are able to read and speak English fluently.
		Overall, writing assessment and evaluation are quite subjective and depend on the skill level of the assessor to determine the accuracy of the results.
		Spelling acquisition is a developmental process much like reading acquisition.
		The Language Experience Approach to the teaching of writing is an effective strategy for writers of all ages and ability levels.

TEACHER *VIGNETTE*

In the fall quarter, a young man named Jorge entered the Literacy Center at the university with his mother. It was his first time on campus, and he was quite excited to be there. Jorge had been going to school in the United States off and on since he was in kindergarten. He was now entering the fifth grade after spending the last two years in school in his home country of Mexico. While Jorge had continuously attended school since he was 5 years old, he had never spent more than one year at a time in U.S. schools and therefore had not become a fluent reader, writer, or speaker of English. In talking with his mother, she stated that they had now permanently relocated to the area and therefore it would be necessary to help Jorge to become fluent in English. Jorge's mother spoke fluent English and Spanish and would be able to support him at home as he acquired English. She wanted to find additional support for him in his literacy skills at the university-based tutorial center.

Richard, a teacher and graduate student at the university, was enrolled in a practicum course in which he would spend 20 hours engaged in one-on-one literacy tutoring. Jorge and Richard would be working together for the quarter. During the first session, Richard spent two hours assessing Jorge's reading, writing, spelling, and oral vocabulary skills. Richard presented Jorge with a picture of a man standing atop a large mountain. They talked for five minutes about what the man was doing up there and what he was thinking. Jorge was able to verbalize his thoughts fairly well, so Richard felt confident he would transfer his thoughts to paper with little difficulty.

After writing for over 15 minutes, Jorge said he was done. Richard asked him to read his story aloud. Jorge didn't hesitate and proceeded to read a fairly detailed story that made sense in relation to the picture. When Richard later looked at the piece of writing, he was shocked. A full page of text was written but was made up of random letter strands. Within the page of writing, the only word that was readable was the word "futbol." Nowhere else on the page was a recognizable word, either in English or Spanish. Instead, it was a jumble of letters with no phonetic or graphically decipherable patterns. How could Jorge read such a rich story aloud when he had written this story?

Richard & Jorge, 2005

Jorge's story is not unlike many others I have heard over the years. He has developed a fairly rich oral vocabulary but has not been able to transfer what he has learned into his writing. Because he has such a strong desire to learn to write, he mimics the writing behaviors he sees modeled in those around him. Jorge seems to have developed an understanding of the syntactic and semantic features of English in relation to speaking, but has yet to be able to encode the language onto the written page. This is quite frustrating for him and for his teacher. Richard wants to assess Jorge's written language ability to determine where the disconnect is located so that he can provide Jorge with meaningful instruction. The next section will provide an overview of the assessments available in the areas of writing conventions, spelling, and content development. To begin with, let's address the area of spelling.

Developmental Assessment of Spelling

ORTHOGRAPHIC KNOWLEDGE:
A learner's level of spelling knowledge; the ability to appropriately connect the letters of the alphabet in the proper sequence in order to form words (Bear, Invernizzi, Templeton, & Johnston, 2004, p. 2). The development of orthographic knowledge is contingent upon the learner's ability to blend and segment sounds, distinguish between different sounds, understand the meaning of words and word parts, and to identify and discriminate between word and sound patterns. Reading and writing are integral components in the development of orthographic knowledge.

In recent years, attitudes have been changing about the nature of spelling assessment and instruction. Often referred to in the literature as **orthographic knowledge**, our understandings of spelling development have undergone serious modification since the work of Charles Read was published in 1971. Read's seminal research study on invented spelling showed that preschoolers actually formulated a logical approach to spelling based on their early understandings of sound-symbol correspondences. What initially resembled scribbling was found to contain relevant aspects denoting some degree of phonetic understanding. Subsequent research has focused on the developmental aspects of invented (or, as I call it, phonetic) spelling across time. Certain patterns have emerged in the research that support the notion of the developmental nature of spelling acquisition (Beers & Henderson, 1977; Gentry, 1981; Henderson; 1990; Templeton & Bear, 1992).

Over time, Henderson (1974, cited in Bear, Invernizzi, Templeton, & Johnston, 2004, p. 10) refined the steps involved in the development of conventional spelling. He labeled the five stages as follows: (1) emergent spelling, (2) letter name-alphabetic spelling, (3) within-word pattern, (4) syllables and affixes, and (5) derivational relations. Within each stage, unique spelling patterns are apparent that appear with increasing levels of complexity. The next section will detail the characteristics of each stage.

EMERGENT SPELLING

Spellers in the emergent stage are beginning to experiment with the written word through the use of pictures, scribbles, and attempts at creating letters, and later, words. It is during this stage of spelling development that children begin to understand some of the conventions of print such as directionality (left to right in English) and sound-symbol correspondences. In the latter portion of this stage, children may leave spaces between letters in an attempt to form words with the intention of relaying a message to the reader.

Students develop orthographic knowledge along a developmental continuum beginning with pictures, scribbles, and strings of letters before moving into words and sentences.

LETTER NAME-ALPHABETIC SPELLING

The letter name-alphabetic stage of spelling development is when children make a tremendous amount of growth in their knowledge of the orthographic features of written language. Generally divided into three parts—early, middle, and late—this stage corresponds to a child's continuing growth as a writer. Not only are children spelling more words conventionally, but they are also able to form complete sentences with correct syntactic features. Teachers will see the children move from the use of simple CVC words into words with consonant blends and digraphs. It is an exciting time for children because they can see their thoughts develop into self-created texts.

WITHIN-WORD PATTERN SPELLING

"Students entering the within word pattern spelling stage have a sight reading vocabulary of 200 to 400 words" (Bear, Invernizzi, Templeton, & Johnston, 2004, p. 15). Students are now engaged in independent reading and writing activities that allow them to further expand their sight reading and writing vocabulary. They are beginning to experiment with irregular spelling patterns such as *–ight* and *–tion*, although they do not always spell these words conventionally.

SYLLABLES AND AFFIXES STAGE

By stage four, students are fairly fluent readers and writers. They are beginning to read and write using differing text structures and have an expanded understanding of the conventions of writing. Students are able to analyze and generalize orthographic patterns to new words. Much of their writing vocabulary now consists of multisyllabic words that require them to "chunk" the words to spell them.

DERIVATIONAL RELATIONS STAGE

The final stage of spelling development often begins in middle school or high school and continues on through adulthood (Bear, Invernizzi, Templeton, & Johnston, 2004). Not all spellers achieve this level of proficiency because of its complexity. Often words that fall within this stage are quite complex and may not follow rules common to the English language. Many of the words have Greek or Latin roots, further complicating their spelling. Spellers who reach this level of proficiency generally have grasped the complexities of the written language of English and may write in several textual genres.

By understanding the developmental nature of writing, and subsequently spelling, teachers are more able to provide appropriate instruction for students. This is especially crucial for ELLs who are not only mastering a new culture and language, but are also learning new syntactical, grammatical, and spelling structures. I am often amazed at the abilities of ELLs as they make their way through the maze we call the English language.

Developmental Assessment of Spelling and Orthographic Knowledge

Based on the developmental nature of spelling acquisition, it becomes essential to find an assessment that is able to determine an ELL's orthographic knowledge level. By determining this level, a teacher will be able to determine the most appropriate spelling words to match the student's developmental level. Very few assessments are able to meet these criteria. Discussions of those that are beneficial follow.

THE QUALITATIVE SPELLING INVENTORY (QSI)

The *Qualitative Spelling Inventory* or *QSI* was created in order to accurately assess a student's level of orthographic knowledge. The *QSI* has varying forms depending on the age level, language, and content area being studied. Overall, each list of spelling words is divided into five blocks, one corresponding to each of the spelling levels identified in the last section. Students are given five words to spell from each stage and are stopped once they miss three of the five spelling words. Teachers are instructed to read the word, use it in a predetermined sentence, and read the word again. This is so that the students have a context for the word as they begin to spell it. Once students have completed the test, the teacher uses the feature guide to determine the features that are present and missing for any given spelling stage. By studying these features, the teacher is able to select the appropriate level for instruction and subsequently choose word study activities to enhance each student's ability. It is a very powerful instructional assessment because it is tied so closely to learning. The *QSI* was developed by Bear, Invernizzi, Templeton, and Johnston (1996) to provide students with hands-on, meaningful, and appropriately leveled spelling instruction. A special feature of the *QSI* is that it offers teachers a Spanish language version called *Inventario Ortográfico en Español* (2004). This version uses culturally relevant spelling words that fit into the same five developmental spelling stages. All versions of the *QSI* can be found in their book *Words Their Way* (Bear, Invernizzi, Templeton, & Johnston, 2004).

SPELLING OBSERVATIONS

While the QSI provides teachers with a structured format for assessing spelling development, teachers can use more informal measures as well. Peter Johnston (1997) suggests that teachers can accurately locate a student's spelling development level by reflecting on several pieces of the student's writing and asking him or her to respell the words under "different conditions." Johnston created a chart in which he wrote the conventional spelling of a word, the "spelling while composing" version of the word, and the "spelling on request" version of the word (see Table 8.1). By asking the student to rewrite the word on request, he found an increased level of proficiency within the student's writing (Johnston, 1997, pp. 153–154). Look at the examples in Table 8.1 to see the qualitative differences in a student's spelling under the two different circumstances.

As you can see from the sample in Table 8.1, the student was able to create more graphically and phonetically similar spellings of each of the words when asked to spell them on demand. Johnston (1997) emphasizes the need for "on-demand" spelling of some words in order to develop an accurate picture of the student's strengths and needs. It also allows teachers to target specific areas for each student. By individualizing the process of teaching spelling by providing more developmentally appropriate instruction, ELLs—and all students for that matter—will become more proficient spellers.

Developmental Assessment of Written Language

Our discussion of spelling naturally leads into the area of writing, although our focus will be on content as well as conventions. To begin with, I will introduce a variety of writing assessments that can be used to accurately evaluate the ELL's writing ability. Again, I will begin with the more formal and standardized assessments before moving into the informal or less structured assessments. The chapter will then end with a list of

TABLE 8.1   Sample Spelling Chart for Differing Circumstances

Conventional Spelling	Draft Spelling	On-Request Spelling
street	strt	stret
house	hows	hous
liked	likt	liked

strategies that can be incorporated into the classroom to support ELLs as they grow as writers in English.

TEST OF EARLY WRITTEN LANGUAGE (TEWL-2)

The *Test of Early Written Language-2 (TEWL-2;* Hresko, Herron, & Peak, 1996) was developed as a means of assessing a younger student's skills (ages 4.0 – 10.11) as an emerging and early writer. While it was not specifically geared toward the ELL, it does provide information on a ELL's ability to write in English. It is also a standardized, norm-referenced test that allows for comparisons across student populations.

The *TEWL-2* is divided into the following two subtests: (1) the basic writing quotient and (2) the contextual writing quotient. By combining the scores for each section, teachers will be able to determine a student's global writing quotient. The basic writing quotient is a measurement of a student's ability to spell conventionally and construct basic sentences with proper capitalization and punctuation; it measures metacognitive abilities in relationship to writing. The contextual writing quotient is a measure of the student's ability to create meaningful, cohesive sentences with a theme, appropriate story structure, and some detail. It will provide the teacher with baseline data on an ELL and help to demonstrate the student's strengths and areas of need in written language.

TEST OF WRITTEN LANGUAGE-3 (TOWL-3)

For those students ages 7.6 to 17.11, the *Test of Written Language–3 (TOWL-3;* Hammill & Larsen, 1996) is the more appropriate of the two standardized tests for measuring written language skills. The test takes approximately 90 minutes to administer and may be given to individual students, small groups, or whole groups. For the purposes of obtain pre- and posttest scores, the test contains two equivalent versions. The *TOWL-3* contains an open-ended writing sample based on a picture prompt that is scored for contextual conventions (capitalization, punctuation, and spelling), contextual language (vocabulary, syntax, and grammar), and story construction (plot, character development, and overall writing ability). In addition to the writing sample, there are five "contrived formats" for assessing writing that include the following components: (a) vocabulary, (b) spelling, (c) style, (d) logical sentences, and (e) sentence combining. Teachers may give all sections of the test or as subtests depending on the students' needs. Because it is norm-referenced, age and gender comparisons can be made. Teachers can use this information to plan instruction throughout the school year and then measure growth by readministering it at the end of the year. It should be seen as an assessment that provides both baseline and summative information. In order to collect formative data, the following assessments would be more appropriate.

ASSESSMENT WITHIN THE WRITER'S WORKSHOP FORMAT

Formative and developmentally appropriate writing assessment is naturally intertwined within sound writing instruction. For that reason, the use of writing rubrics, writing conferences, peer, and self-evaluation should all be addressed within the framework of writer's workshop. Freeman and Freeman (1998) state that "A workshop approach to writing is especially successful with students whose first language is not English. Students can choose what is important to them, and the students' messages are accepted and valued even when the form is not completely conventional" (p. 92). That statement

Spelling and written language assessment can take place within the context of the writer's workshop format by engaging the students in reflection and self-assessment.

lends powerful support to the use of writer's workshop within all classrooms, especially those containing ELLs. It is through writer's workshop that students are given a voice with which to express their ideas, beliefs, and desires, and with the creation of such meaningful texts, students can develop writing fluency.

What Does Writer's Workshop Look Like?

Lucy Calkins (1994) wrote a wonderful text called *The Art of Teaching Writing,* in which she described all of the parts and pieces needed to encourage students to write within a workshop format. To begin with, it is important to "establish a predictable environment" for writing (p. 183). In doing so, teachers will want to set up the physical environment of the classroom to enable students to have easy access to writing materials, books and other resources, and their writing portfolios. Students also need a space in which to write where they feel comfortable and can collaborate with the teacher and their peers. This may include a mix of table space and floor space in which to move around. Additionally, students will need to *know* that a certain amount of time is dedicated to writing at set points throughout the week. These times are built into the schedule to show the importance of writing.

Once the room environment is established and a schedule has been developed, it is time to introduce the students to the process of engaging in writer's workshop. Within the structure of writer's workshop, Calkins (1986) has established the following essential components: (a) minilessons for needed small group instruction, (b) work time for writing and conferring, (c) peer conferencing and response group time, (d) share sessions for an informal sharing of a piece of writing, and (e) publication celebration in which writers are encouraged to share their writing with peers, family, and friends (pp. 189-191). Within this structure lies the freedom to explore various genres of writing as well as topics of interest to the writer. It is here that ELLs will experience success and independence, along with instructional support. It is a win–win situation if implemented correctly and with consistency.

What Does Assessment Look Like within the Writer's Workshop Format?

Assessment can take many forms in the writer's workshop. It involves continuous self-reflection, peer reflection, and teacher reflection. Often students assess themselves and their peers using feedback forms (see Figures 8.1 and 8.2) and checklists (see Figure 8.3). Figure 8.1 is an example of a feedback form that I have used with students for the past decade. It has been revised along the way, but it serves to help students to reflect on the strengths and weaknesses in a piece of writing. Notice that students are always asked to initially look for strengths before addressing the weaknesses. This small requirement has allowed students (and teachers) to be able to identify the strengths in any piece of writing.

Both the self-evaluation and peer evaluation forms can be placed in the student's portfolio along with the composition. They can also be used as a starting point for the

FIGURE 8.1   Writing Self-Assessment Form

Author's Name: _____

Date: _____

Title of Composition: _____

Genre of Composition: _____

What are three things you like about your composition?

What are three things you could do to improve this composition?

What is the name of your peer evaluator?

What do you want your peer evaluator to review in this composition?

writer's conference to be held with the teacher. Forms can be modified to include more complex or simple language depending on the age level of the students.

Prior to asking students to evaluate their writing or the writing of a peer, it may be beneficial to have them review their composition using an editor's checklist (see Figure 8.3). The checklists are age and grade specific, so it would be best to brainstorm a list of items to be included on the checklist with your students. This will not only allow you to check their level of understanding related to the content and conventions needed to create a good piece of writing, but it also makes them aware of the standards by

FIGURE 8.2   Peer Evaluation Form (on reverse side of the self-evaluation form)

Peer Evaluator's Name: _____

Date: _____

Title of Composition: _____

Time Spent Reviewing Writing: _____

Name and describe three things you like about this compositon:

Describe three things that would make this composition even better:

Additional comments:

FIGURE 8.3   Sample Intermediate Level Editor's Checklist

Editor's Checklist for Expository Texts:

1. Did I begin each sentence with a capital letter and end each with the appropriate punctuation mark? _____

2. Did I create a new paragraph for each new idea? _____

3. Did I indent each new paragraph? _____

4. Does each paragraph have a topic sentence and at least four supporting sentences? _____

5. Did I add a transitional sentence between one new idea and another? _____

6. Did I edit my writing to be sure it made sense and make any needed corrections? _____

7. Did I write a powerful opening statement that will grab the reader's attention? _____

8. Did I proofread my paper and correct my spelling errors? _____

9. You are now ready to self-evaluate your composition and then have a peer evaluate it.

which they will assess themselves and their peers. The checklist found in Figure 8.3 was developed by intermediate-level students for a piece of expository text.

At this point, the writer should feel more comfortable asking a peer to evaluate his or her writing. It would also be helpful to model the various facets of the assessment and evaluation process prior to asking students to participate independently.

If you would like to add an additional level of formative assessment, you may want to delve into the 6-Traits work done by Vicki Spandel. Spandel has written a book entitled *Creating Writers Through 6-Trait Writing Assessment and Instruction* (2001). In this book she details a more systematic way of teaching writing in which the students are exposed to the 6-Traits that are present in a good piece of writing. The 6-Traits are as follows: (1) ideas, (2) organization, (3) voice, (4) word choice, (5) sentence fluency, and (6) conventions and presentation. While Spandel was not the first to identify the traits of good writing, she was a driving force in infusing these traits into a workshop environment.

Spandel (2001) has detailed how to implement the 6-Traits into writing by first exposing students to books that richly demonstrate one or more of the 6-Traits. For example, when teaching students about the concept of voice within a piece of writing, you will want to bring in works by various authors whose voices shine through in their writing. An example for intermediate level students might be a book written by Judy Blume or the poetry of Langston Hughes. For younger students, you may want to introduce them to Shel Silverstein or Patricia Polacco. While each author writes using distinctively different styles, you can hear each author's voice talking to you through the words on the page. It will be through modeling, practice, and feedback that your students develop as writers. This becomes even more important for ELLs as they begin to understand the varying styles of writing that exist within the English language. English tends to be more linear, while some other languages may have a more circular style of writing. It will help ELLs to have access to some of these "secrets" of writing in English.

Building upon the 6-Traits of writing instruction is the use of ongoing assessment by way of **analytical** and **holistic rubrics**. Sample rubrics can be found in the appendix section of the text.

Regardless of the type or types of assessment teachers use in their classrooms, it is important for the ELL to be able to be assessed and evaluated fairly. It is suggested that teachers of ELLs not only obtain a baseline writing sample in English, but that they also have the student write on a topic of choice or using a prompt in his or her native language. By having a native speaker evaluate the piece of text, a teacher will be able to accurately determine which conventions the student has mastered in the primary language so they can be built upon in during English language instruction.

ANALYTIC WRITING RUBRIC:
An analytic rubric contains a description of specific standards, conventions, traits, or areas of focus for scoring a piece of writing. It allows the assessor to break down a piece of writing into component areas and locate the strengths and needs within each area. It generally provides the assessor with a series of numerical values on a 0-5 (or other) range.

HOLISTIC WRITING RUBRIC:
A holistic writing rubric allows the assessor to judge the entire piece of writing as a whole. It looks at its overall effectiveness and quality (Gunning, 2002).

Strategies to Build Written Language Development

Several outstanding strategies are listed that can be added to the classroom in order to provide ELLs with a safe and supportive environment in which to express themselves with written language:

- Writing think-alouds
- Language Experience Approach
- Daily news story
- Shared and interactive writing
- Cut-up sentence journals
- Alternate writing
- Color-coded writing
- Silent Sustained Writing (SSW)
- Peer conferencing and response groups
- Word study activities
- Individualized spelling lists
- Word walls
- Speller's workshop
- Framed rhyming innovations
- Writer's workshop

REVISITING THE *CHAPTER ANTICIPATION GUIDE*

Spend a few minutes reviewing the statements presented in the Chapter Anticipation Guide at the beginning of the chapter. Compare your notes with those **highlighted**.

End-of-the-Chapter Anticipation Guide

Agree	Disagree	Statement
	✗	Spelling and vocabulary essentially require identical skills and therefore, identical instructional techniques. *False—Vocabulary words are words that teachers want students to be able to read and define to increase comprehension of a particular text. Spelling is a developmental process linked to writing acquisition that is developmental in nature. Students learn to read and spell words so they can be used in their writing.*

Agree	Disagree	Statement
	✗	ELLs should not receive instruction in writing until they are able to read and speak English fluently. *False—Since English-only students begin to draw, scribble, and write as they are learning to read, ELLs can do the same. Reading and writing are compatible processes that enrich one another.*
✗	✗	Overall, writing assessment and evaluation are quite subjective and depend on the skill level of the assessor to determine the accuracy of the results. *Hmmm . . . writing assessment can be made to be quite objective by using analytic rubrics and standardized tests like the TOWL-3 and the TEWL-2. While this is the case, some aspects of writing have been difficult to assess.*
✗		Spelling acquisition is a developmental process much like reading acquisition. **True—Spelling is quite developmental and therefore should be assessed and instructed that way as well.**
	✗	The Language Experience Approach to the teaching of writing is an effective strategy for writers of all ages and ability levels. *False—The LEA is a strategy whereby a student dictates a story to the teacher as the teacher records it on paper. It is a wonderful strategy to use with students who are at the early or emergent stage of writing. It would be helpful for ELLs just beginning to write in English.*

ASSESSMENT *TOOLKIT*

Writing

Individual or small group assessing:

- *Test of Written Language-3 (TOWL-3)* for grades, and the *Test of Early Written Language-2 (TEWL-2)* for grades.
- Writing conferences based on a self-selected piece of writing from the writer's portfolio.
- Self-assessment/peer assessment form and a writing sample.
- Analytic and/or holistic scoring rubrics based on the 6-Traits of writing (Spandel, 2004).

Whole class assessing:

- Chart paper, markers, and group-constructed story during shared, guided, and/or interactive writing session.

ASSESSMENT *TOOLKIT*

Spelling

Individual or small group assessing:

- *Appropriate level of the Qualitative Spelling Inventory* (QSI; Bear, Johnston, Templeton, & Invernizzi, 2004) in English and Spanish for those ELLs whose native language is Spanish.
- *Writing Vocabulary Assessment* (Clay, 1993, 2002).

Whole group assessing:

- Blank paper, pencils, student journals.
- *McGuffey Developmental Spelling Inventory.*
- Writing prompt or free writing sample.

Assessment in the Content Areas

Read through each of the following statements prior to reading the chapter. Place a checkmark in either the box labeled "agree" or "disagree" depending upon whether you believe the statement to be true or false. As you read the chapter, refer back to the chart and confirm or modify your initial responses.

Initial Chapter Anticipation Guide

Agree	Disagree	Statement
		When students are fluent in their primary language, they often bring well-developed higher level thinking skills to their content area classes.
		Graphic organizers are excellent tools for organizing information, but are rarely useful for assessing students' growth.
		The Frayer Model helps students to learn new content area vocabulary and distinguish between essential and non-essential information.
		By the time ELLs and their peers enter middle school, they should realize that reading and writing are tools for learning valuable information.
		Instruction and assessment are two discrete learning processes.

TEACHER *VIGNETTE*

Leila was a graduate student in a summer course taking place in Hawai'i. It was a year-long program for middle school and high school teachers who were interested in earning a reading endorsement on their single subject teaching certificate. Leila had taught middle school social studies on the big island for the past twelve years and had found that many of her native Hawaiian students were experiencing difficulty in her classes. For the most part, her students spoke very little Hawaiian but did use what it referred to Hawaiian Creole or Pidgin English. As a social studies teacher, she had only been required to take one reading methods course and that had been several years ago. Wanting to help her students read the texts and enjoy the content of the class, she had joined this year-long endorsement program to enhance her skills as a teacher. Leila expressed concern that her students were unable to comprehend the grade-level reading materials and often wrote stilted essays for her class. Many had a great deal of difficulty learning the content area vocabulary and found that their grades were suffering.

Realizing that the native Hawaiian students seemed to have even more difficulty than their Japanese peers, Leila had to find out how to prevent her students from dropping out of school once they reached high school. At times the issues seemed overwhelming, but she was determined to help them to succeed in their content area classes by teaching them how to learn and appropriate content area vocabulary into their reading and writing. She also believed they needed instruction in the use of content area reading strategies in order to increase their level of comprehension. During our time together, Leila focused on studying meaningful assessment and instruction across the content areas. Some of what she found has been incorporated into the following chapter.

Leila, eighth grade social studies teacher

Content Area Assessment and Instruction

From Leila's story, it is apparent that while her students were not considered to be ELLs, many of them did not use what educators refer to as Standard English. **Standard English** is the mainstream English used by the majority of the population of English-speaking countries. Teachers often call this type of English "book English." Leila found that many of her students had a limited vocabulary level and often had not been exposed to a wealth of reading materials in their homes. By the time they entered middle school, many of the students were years behind their standard English–speaking peers. Concerned with their academic and economic future, Leila wanted to empower her students so they would feel successful in school by improving their skills and content-

STANDARD ENGLISH:
A long debated concept since the inception of the United States, Standard English is generally seen as the standard language used in the educational system. This form of English is generally more formal and can be found in most textbooks, dictionaries, and academic discourse communities (Durkin, 1995).

area knowledge. By becoming more successful in school, she realized that they would be more likely to go on to college. Leila's story may sound very similar to stories you have heard or experienced yourselves.

It is essential that teachers find ways to assess their students across the content areas using culturally and linguistically fair measures. Modifications need to be made for ELLs because they are not only learning content area information, but they are also acquiring conversational and academic language. Zwiers (2004) states that many second language students who are literate in their primary languages "have developed abilities in mental multitasking and hierarchically written information. Reading in their first language has challenged them to think in complex ways and to process texts quickly"(p. 7). By assessing their primary and secondary language skills first, as described in previous chapters, teachers will be able to determine the best course of action for each student. There is no need to focus on early literacy skills and concepts when these have been well developed in their first language. It now becomes time to focus on assessing their content area abilities and building their content area literacy strategies and content area knowledge.

Teachers often informally assess a student's literacy skills through the use of content area learning strategies such as learning logs, graphic organizers, and questioning strategies.

This chapter will focus on alternative assessments that will prove beneficial to ELLs within the context of the classroom. For practical purposes, the best assessments are those that are embedded within the instruction so as not to take time away from the actual academic content. For the purposes of this text, we'll focus on the area of social studies and science.

Content Area Vocabulary Assessment

Social studies is a subject that requires students to read complex, fact-based texts and remember important events, eras, and historical figures. In itself, this can be very trying for English-only students, but it can be overwhelming for second language students. One of the main components of social studies is the development of vocabulary related to the topic of study. The same holds true for science. Much of the reading done in science contains a multitude of vocabulary words that must be mastered in order to understand the concepts in any depth. While Chapter 4 begins the discussion of oral vocabulary assessment techniques that can be transferred to the content areas, further discussion of content area vocabulary is warranted within this chapter.

GRAPHIC ORGANIZERS

One of the most useful techniques for assessing vocabulary within the content areas is through the use of graphic organizers or mind maps. Graphic organizers help students to arrange information into meaningful units containing significant facts and vocabulary words. They can be used to assess prior knowledge before beginning a unit of study and then again to determine how much the student has learned across time. "Students' ways of thinking, interpreting, and organizing text information into graphic organizers often prove to be very innovative and insightful. You can make rubrics or checklists that go with the graphics to be used" (Zwiers, 2004, p. 18).

For example, if a student has been asked to read a chapter on the human musculoskeletal system, it would be useful to have him or her create a "spider map" (see Figure 9.1) prior to participating in the unit of study. Figure 9.1 shows a preinstruction mind map created by Devon, an eighth-grade student. In it he was asked to place the topic of study in the center of the map and then put in appropriate anatomy vocabulary and knowledge in the "legs" of the spider. This map was created four weeks before he completed the science unit.

As you can see from his map, Devon understands the role muscles play in movement but is not familiar with the names and locations of specific muscles. He also understands that exercise promotes the growth and subsequent strength of muscles. Interestingly, he is familiar with some of the harmful effects of steroid use on the body and realizes that steroids are often used by athletes to enhance their performance. This provides his science teacher with useful information that needs to be addressed and/or

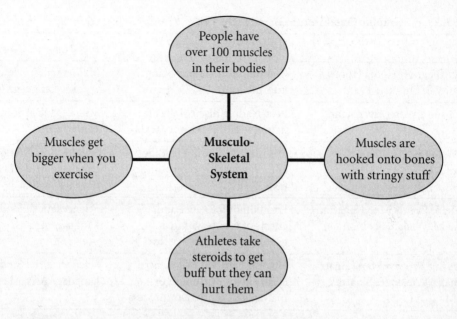

FIGURE 9.1   Devon's Initial Spider Graphic Organizer

clarified as the class studies the musculoskeletal system. Devon's teacher will ask him to repeat this task at the end of the unit of study to check his understanding, and then he will reteach as needed.

One of the advantages to using graphic organizers as assessment tools is that they are fairly simple to use, there are a variety of graphic organizers to fit the different needs and content areas, and they provide a visual representation of the information that can then be used as a prewriting activity. They can also be used as a study guide for exams.

In addition to the spider map, Table 9.1 on page 132 lists other types of graphic organizers and the content areas in which they are best suited. While this list does not cover all of those available, it provides a sampling of some of the most popular types of graphic organizers in use.

These organizers will help ELLs to organize new content area information along with the vocabulary necessary for success in their classes. We will next discuss the Frayer Model of Vocabulary Instruction, building upon the use of graphic organizers is the use of learning logs across the content areas.

THE FRAYER MODEL

The Frayer Model of Vocabulary Instruction (Frayer, Frederick, & Klausmeir, 1969) has been in use since the 1960s. While it is generally seen as an instructional strategy, it

TABLE 9.1   Graphic Organizers as Assessment Tools

Type	Purpose	Useful Content Areas
Venn Diagram Hoola Hoops (Cooter & Thomas, 1998)	Comparing and contrasting information	Mathematics, Science, Social Studies, Language Arts
Discussion Web (Alvermann, 1991)	Post-reading discussions of narrative and expository texts	Science, Social Studies, Language Arts
K-W-L-Q (Ogle, 1986; Sinatra, 1997)	Pre-reading, During reading and Post-reading of expository texts	Science, Social Studies, Language Arts, Mathematics
Chain of Events Map (Sinatra, Gemake, Wielan, & Sinatra, 1998)	Location of the cause and effects of events within an expository or narrative text.	Science, Social Studies, Language Arts
Steps in a Process Map (Sinatra, Gemake, Wielan, & Sinatra, 1998)	Helping clarify the sequential events in a story, event, or mathematical problem/process.	Science, Social Studies, Language Arts, Mathematics

is just as effective as a content area vocabulary assessment. Although it was initially envisioned as a science vocabulary strategy, it works quite well in social studies and mathematics as an assessment and instructional tool. The purpose of the Frayer Model is to have students find essential attributes of a particular concept along with nonessential attributes. This helps them to discuss the concepts that are most important. Initially, the teacher provides the students with the essential and nonessential concepts and examples that match each. As the students take on more of the responsibility for the task, they work individually or with partners to complete the activity. The model can act as an assessment of what the students have learned after studying a particular topic or concept or as a pre- and post-assessment measure. Table 9.2 provides an example of a completed Frayer Model Chart based on the science topic of planets.

CONTENT AREA LEARNING LOGS

Throughout the language arts classroom, literature logs have been used to document students' understanding of a story or to connect the text to personal events or feelings they have related to the story content. These journals have been called by various names: (a) learning logs (Commander & Smith, 1996), (b) reader response journals (Berger, 1996), (c) dialogue journals, (d) literature logs, and others. Regardless of the name given, learning logs are excellent assessment tools in the content areas. Learning logs can be used to predict or hypothesize about a topic that the students will be studying; they can be used to document the knowledge gleaned as students study a topic; and

TABLE 9.2   Example of the Frayer Model

Concept under Study: ___Planets in the Milky Way Solar System___

Essential Information	*Examples*
Orbit around the sun	Saturn
One orbit equals one planet's year	Earth
They each have different atmospheres	Mars

Nonessential Information	*Nonexamples*
Not all planets have rings	Earth's moon
They are different colors	the sun
Found in different sizes	constellations

they can be used by students to summarize their knowledge after reading and studying a topic in science, math, and/or social studies. By keeping a journal of predictions, research, and thoughts, a teacher can gain insight into the student's growth across time and use it to guide subsequent instruction. Learning logs or journals also promote the notion of reading and writing to learn across the content areas. The learning logs can become part of the student's portfolio and may allow the student to use them to reflect on his or her own growth over time. Additionally, learning logs are embedded into the classroom instruction and add to the quality of instruction being provided by content area teachers. Intertwined with genuine reading and writing experiences, learning logs can enrich the educational experience for students as well as illustrate that reading and writing are not separate from science, social studies, and mathematics.

Strategies to Enhance Content Area Instruction

- Reader's workshop
- Writer's workshop
- Reciprocal teaching
- Question-Answer-Response (QAR)
- SQ3R
- Graphic organizers
- Instructional conversations
- K-W-L
- K-W-L-S

- Guided reading
- Read-alouds
- Wide reading
- Group summarizing
- The GIST strategy
- Reader response journals
- Jigsaw
- Mind mapping
- Think-alouds

These are but a few of the strategies that promote content area assessment and instruction. Combined with the information provided in previous chapters, teachers will have a sound repertoire of strategies and assessments for use across all content areas. The assessments and strategies selected are those most useful for second language learners because they involve all of the areas of language arts: reading, writing, listening, speaking, and visual literacy. The more teachers can incorporate all of these areas into their daily instruction, the more successful our second language learners will be when entering schools in which English is the primary language. Ultimately, our goal is to provide all students with an opportunity for meaningful, relevant instruction at the appropriate level.

REVISITING THE *CHAPTER ANTICIPATION GUIDE*

Spend a few minutes reviewing the statements presented in the Chapter Anticipation Guide at the beginning of the chapter. Compare your notes with those **highlighted**.

End-of-the-Chapter Anticipation Guide

Agree	Disagree	Statement
✘		When students are fluent in their primary language, they often bring well-developed higher level thinking skills to their content area classes. *True—Students who are fluent in their primary languages have often developed excellent organizational and higher level thinking skills in the content areas that can be applied to their content area courses delivered in English.*
	✘	Graphic organizers are excellent tools for organizing information, but are rarely useful for assessing students' growth. *False—Graphic organizers are quick and meaningful ways to pretest and posttest students in the content areas.*
✘		The Frayer Model helps students to learn new content area vocabulary and distinguish between essential and nonessential information. *True—Although it is a complex model, it can be quite useful for students when trying to discern important information from nonessential information. This makes it a great studying tool as well.*
✘		By the time ELLs and their peers enter middle school, they should realize that reading and writing are tools for learning valuable information. *True—Students should now be taught that reading and writing have multiple purposes: Helping them to learn and organize valuable content information as well as being a way to express and entertain themselves.*
	✘	Instruction and assessment are two discrete learning processes. *False—Assessment is most valuable when it is integrated into meaningful classroom instruction.*

CHAPTER TEN

Putting the Pieces Together

Read through each of the following statements prior to reading the chapter. Place a checkmark in either the box labeled "agree" or "disagree" depending upon whether you believe the statement to be true or false. As you read the chapter, refer back to the chart and confirm or modify your initial responses.

Initial Chapter Anticipation Guide

Agree	Disagree	Statement
		Student-led parent conferences work best when implemented after grade 3.
		When bringing an interpreter to a conference, it is best to look at the parent rather than the interpreter during the conversation.
		When evaluating assessment results, it is most important to identify the student's areas of need.
		It is unnecessary to maintain both formative and summative portfolios for ELLs and English-only students in the regular classroom.
		Developing assessment-based instructional goals allows teachers to provide relevant instruction on a daily basis.

CLASSROOM *VIGNETTE*

I exited the freeway and took a side street that led to a quaint little schoolhouse located at the apex of three major Los Angeles freeways. The road was blocked off by a metal barrier, forcing me to park in a housing tract near by. The homes were old; many had been built over fifty years ago.

Awaiting me inside the alcove at the front of the school was a friendly face that said "Hello" in newly acquired English. I could see that my greeter was wearing a volunteer badge and seemed quite proud to be there to welcome all of the visitors for that day. I signed in and put on a name tag before heading out to the portable classroom, Room 35A.

When I entered the classroom, I was greeted by a student who asked me my name and asked if I was there to pick up my child. I smiled at the young lady and told her I would be visiting her classroom to see all of the wonderful things that were going on inside its four walls.

Since that August morning three years ago I have spent many hours observing the magic taking place there. The classroom is quite unique. It is a K-2 multiage classroom with forty ELLs and two teachers. While both of the teachers speak Spanish, the instruction takes place in English. Spanish is highly valued but is mainly used when the students are conversing with one another or when the teacher needs to clarify a particularly complex concept. It is a vibrant, student-centered classroom where the students are owners in the learning process. This was never more evident than on the day I spent observing the student-led conferences.

Parents began arriving in groups of three or four right after lunch. I watched as their kindergarten, first-, or second-grade child grabbed them by the hand and led them to a spot on the carpet or a chair in the library. Each child carried a pencil and clipboard as each guided his or her parent(s) to sit down. The clipboard contained a set of directions for a series of activities that they would participate in together during the hour-long conference.

First, each child located his or her book box, selected a book, and read it aloud to the parent(s), stopping to make "connections" every page or two. Next, each child and parent took turns reading entries from the child's journal. Parents were given time to write a note back to their children in the journal. From here they moved to the math area where the child modeled a specific math skill while playing a math game with parents. The conference culminated as each set of parents, child, and teacher sat in a circle to discuss the child's report card and working portfolio.

Throughout the conference process, both teachers rotated around the classroom, providing assistance as needed.

It became apparent that the teacher and students had practiced how to run a conference prior to conference day, and many had previous experience conferencing because they had been in the same class for a total of three years. It was a very relaxing atmosphere in which students were invited to showcase what they had been learning and share the moment with their parents.

In this chapter, I will pull together all of the pieces discussed throughout the book and begin to develop an overall picture of the student as a whole. It can become quite easy to fall into the habit of seeing a child as the sum of all of his or her academic abilities and forget the more emotional and familial influences that impact him or her on a daily basis. When evaluating the assessment results and developing an instructional plan for students, it is essential to bring learners and their parents into the conversation. It was best summed up by Brock and Raphael (2005) when they wrote that "effective teachers of students from diverse backgrounds understand that the students themselves can provide invaluable insights into their thinking, learning, and lives that we, as educators can draw from as we design instruction for them" (p. 6). The learners and their families are an often overlooked resource that can enrich the learning process. By opening up the lines of communication and extending an invitation to parents to visit the classroom, they will feel more comfortable coming to school to actively participate in their children's education. A high degree of comfort and acceptance is necessary for parents to feel welcome at school. Without parental support, children will not have the best educational experience possible.

It is also important to realize that as our society changes, so does the structure of the family. It may be that school-to-home communication needs to take on some different configurations: (a) newsletters, (b) automated phone messages, (c) automated homework assignments available by phone, (d) communication and conferencing via email, (e) video-based lessons and information for parents, (f) weekend conferencing, and (g) student-led conferencing are just some of the options presently being proposed (Allington & Cunningham, 2002; Brantley, 2004). Simply changing the approach to communicating with parents may prove to be quite successful. This is demonstrated nicely in the classroom vignette on page 138.

The vignette details a highly successful conferencing approach that has been in place for nine years at an urban school in California. The K-5 school first opened in 1895 (yes—it is more than 100 years old!) and is still partially housed in the original school building. The school is on a year-round schedule and instructs an average of 1,000 students per school year. Of the 1,000 students, 97.2 percent are Hispanic, 0.1 percent are White, 2.5 percent are Black, and 0.2 percent are Asian. A total of 674 students were classified as ELLs in the 2004–2005 school year. Due to the number of students who qualify for free and reduced lunches, the school has been designated as a Title I school. Because of this designation, the school receives federal funds to provide students with extra assistance in the areas of reading and math, as well as funds to provide family literacy and numeracy workshops for parents and teachers. I have had the good fortune of observing in one of the classrooms at this school for the last three years and have been amazed by the literacy-rich, meaningful instruction taking place on a daily basis. I hope you enjoy this classroom as much as I do!

Developing a Picture of the Whole Student

Through daily work samples, observations, checklists, verbal interactions, and more formalized assessments, teachers have gathered an enormous amount of information on each of the students in their classrooms. While some of the data is quantitative in nature, much of it is qualitative and therefore more difficult to evaluate and summarize. Gredler and Johnson (2004) liken the process of evaluating qualitative assessment results to the approach taken by researchers when they take extensive field notes, collect artifacts, and categorize their findings into domains (Spradley, 1980) for interpretation and analysis. A domain is defined as ". . . a category of cultural meaning that includes smaller categories" (Spradley, 1980, p. 88). As teachers interpret the data, they consider the learning context, form educated hypotheses about the student's learning that are affirmed and disaffirmed throughout the course of the learning process, and summarize the information so that it can be reported to various audiences (Denzin & Lincoln, 1994; Gredler & Johnson, 2004). It should be noted that the process of affirming and disaffirming these educational hypotheses is continuous, thus preventing the misidentification of a student's needs and strengths. It also allows a teacher to keep

Teachers use a variety of qualitative information to make daily instructional decisions for all students.

an open mind about a student to prevent unnecessary labeling. By taking such a holistic approach to instruction, teachers are more likely to develop a more meaningful educational program for each student. The first step in "whole student" or holistic assessment is to identify each student's areas of strength and need.

Identification of Strengths and Needs

When a teacher has collected sufficient evidence regarding a student's performance across a variety of classroom contexts and through multiple data sources, it is then time to ferret out the relevant pieces of information on which to base educational decisions (Hiebert, Valencia, & Afflerbach, 1994). This process involves the systematic search for performance patterns. By relying on data collected across time and contexts, a teacher can then detect patterns that show a student's "typical" level of performance (Gredler & Johnson, 2004). This process decreases the likelihood that a teacher will misjudge a student's abilities.

In reviewing the assessment data, a teacher will be able to construct domains based on the patterns identified. These domains should consist of a student's strengths and needs across all areas of language arts. Table 10.1 is representative of a tool that can be used as the teacher evaluates the information collected, keeping in mind that it is a dynamic tool that can be continually updated.

The language arts categories found in Table 10.1 can be modified to match the areas specific to a given grade level. A separate chart can be developed for a student based on the results of his or her primary language assessments and secondary language assessments as well. Note the fourth column on the table. It provides a space for the teacher to begin to brainstorm teaching strategies and activities that would be beneficial to the student. This will be addressed in more detail in the next section.

Development of Appropriate Assessment-Based Instructional Goals

Once the student's areas of strength and need have been identified, the next step is to create a series of realistic, meaningful learning goals. These goals will serve as the foundation for all instruction for the ELL. Reflecting back upon the vignette presented at the beginning of the chapter, active involvement of the student in this process is imperative. While it is much easier to conference with an older student as you review assessment results and develop learning goals, this same conferencing can be done with younger students as well. It will just require a modification of the language used while conferencing and the complexity of the goals developed. It is amazing how aware students are of their needs and their strengths at all ages and developmental levels. I have often been surprised by this during my years of teaching various grade levels. During

TABLE 10.1   Strengths and Needs Analysis Chart

Areas of Language Arts	Strength Domains	Need Domains	Instructional Implications (Strategies)
Receptive Vocabulary			
Expressive Vocabulary			
Concepts of Print			
Phonemic Awareness			
Phonics			
Reading Fluency			
Word Recognition (in context)			
Word Recognition (in isolation)			
Reading Comprehension— Narrative			
Reading Comprehension— Expository			
Spelling			
Written Language			

LEARNING GOAL:
A goal that is specific to one particular student and is based the student's strengths and needs. Learning goals are dynamic and cumulative and should be modified as needed based on the student's assessment results. Learning goals are clearly stated so they can be measured using both quantitative and qualitative assessment measures. Learning goals can refer to academic and affective learning strengths and needs (Maxim, 1999).

the goals conference, it is the teacher's role to guide the student and clarify the results as needed. Table 10.1 can be used to stimulate the conversation by providing the student with concrete evidence of his or her performance, leading into a conversation regarding the development of **learning goals**.

Learning goals should be very specific and lead to increased student achievement and improved classroom instruction. They serve to help the teacher and learner focus on developmentally appropriate lessons and facilitate scaffolded learning. Figure 10.1 provides examples of learning goals developed for two different ELLs, Jaime and Lourdes.

As you can see from the examples of learning goals given in Figure 10.1, each goal has several components. Multiple components are needed in order to clarify the exact nature of the learning goal. Without such clarity it becomes impossible to locate appropriate instructional strategies and to find the appropriate means of assessing progress. In the next section, I will refer back to the learning goals in Figure 10.1 when discussing instructional strategies.

FIGURE 10.1   Example of Learning Goals for Jaime and Lourdes

1. Jaime comprehends a grade-level narrative story in English:

    a. Jaime can retell the story in its proper sequence.

    b. Jaime can restate the problem and resolution.

    c. Jaime can name and describe the main characters.

    d. Jaime can describe the setting of the story.

2. Lourdes will fluently read a short nonfiction article at her independent reading level:

    a. Lourdes can accurately decode the words in the article using a variety of word recognition strategies.

    b. Lourdes will be able to define vocabulary using context clues.

    c. Lourdes will be able to accurately summarize the main concepts in the article.

    d. Lourdes will be able to read the article at the appropriate reading rate and with expression.

Providing Relevant Assessment-Based Classroom Instruction

Once the learning goals have been identified and subsequently broken down into meaningful components, it is time to determine the most appropriate instructional strategies, materials, activities, and assessments for the ELL. As an example, let's refer to Lourdes from Figure 10.1.

LOURDES

Lourdes is a seventh-grade student whose native language is Portuguese. She has been educated in the United States since the fifth grade. Prior to moving to the United States, Lourdes was an A and B student in Brazil who could decode and comprehend narrative and expository texts in Portuguese at grade level. Since moving to the United States, she has been able to learn English fairly quickly, although she is having difficulty in her content area courses because of the specific vocabulary needed to read expository texts successfully. Based on assessment results, the following learning goals have been developed by her language arts teacher (see Figure 10.2). Underneath each goal is a list of possible strategies to support Lourdes' classroom instruction in the hopes she will master these goals.

Because so many strategies can be used to achieve the learning goals set for Lourdes, it is time to consider her learning style and strengths when selecting the most appropriate means of instruction. Because some of these strategies are incorporated into her daily classroom lessons, a cycle of continual assessment and evaluation should be maintained. By regularly assessing Lourdes, it will be simple to adjust her instruction as needed, allowing for her growth spurts and lags. It might be necessary to reevaluate the use of a particular strategy if she seems to be losing ground in some area of the curriculum. One of the best ways to keep track of her progress is through the use of portfolios and teacher–student conferences.

Literacy Portfolios and Portfolio Conferences

The portfolio is built on the underlying belief that literacy learning is enjoyable and has practical and personal significance. Quality literacy instruction employs methods that are interesting, dynamic, and compelling and results from the teacher's understanding of what strategies students use in daily encounters with print, what students enjoy reading, and what is meaningful to students. As students become proficient in reading and writing, they increase opportunities for both academic and personal success. (Cohen & Wiener, 2003, p. 91)

FIGURE 10.2   Examples of Expanded Learning Goals for Lourdes

2. Lourdes will fluently read a short nonfiction article at her independent reading level:

   a. Lourdes can accurately decode the words in the article using a variety of word recognition strategies.

   b. Lourdes will be able to define vocabulary using context clues.

   Strategies to Support Goals (a) and (b):

   - Context clues
   - Chunking
   - Onsets and rimes
   - Morphemic analysis
   - Structural analysis
   - Wide reading
   - Word study activities
   - Repeated readings
   - Personal word walls

   c. Lourdes will be able to accurately summarize the main concepts in the article.

   Strategies to Support Goal (c):

   - Anticipation guides
   - DRTA & DLTA
   - QAR
   - Graphic organizers
   - Oral and written retellings
   - Reciprocal teaching
   - SQ4R
   - Learning logs
   - K-W-L-Q
   - Paragraph frames

   d. Lourdes will be able to read the article at the appropriate reading rate and with expression.

   Strategies to Support Goal (d):

   - Reader's theater and creative drama
   - Neurological Impress Method
   - Repeated readings
   - Interrupted improv role-play
   - Choral and guided reading
   - Mini shared reading
   - Language Experience Approach

PORTFOLIO:

A selective collection of a learner's work across time. "Its principal purpose is to tell a story of a learner's growth in proficiency, long-term achievement, and significant accomplishments in a given area" (Borich & Tombari, 2004, p. 229). Portfolios can be formative, showing the learner's understanding of a concept or process at a given time. Portfolios can also be summative and demonstrate a learner's understanding at the end of a unit, grading period, or school year.

Literacy **portfolios** can be powerful tools to measure success and growth for all students, especially ELLs. I say this because ELLs are often assessed using more informal means that are difficult to quantify in a simple format. Literacy portfolios allow the teacher and ELL to work together to set literacy goals based on a multitude of assessments and modify them as needed. Within the portfolio conference, the student can reflect upon his or her progress and actively participate in the modification of these literacy goals. Together, the teacher and student are actively engaged in a meaningful discussion based on products created by the student. These "products" can be in the form of standardized tests, written compositions, audio- and videotapes, content area work samples, journal entries, self- and peer-reflection sheets, field notes, checklists, and a plethora of other artifacts. It is the combination of the artifacts that paints a picture of the student's areas of strength and need and lends itself to the development of goals.

Think of a portfolio as a recursive process in which a student and teacher participate throughout the year, and even year to year, to support the student's academic and social achievement. Viewing the portfolios and the conferences as a continual process takes away some of the pressure to have "perfect" samples in the portfolios. Instead, portfolios are reflective of the continual growth made by a student across time.

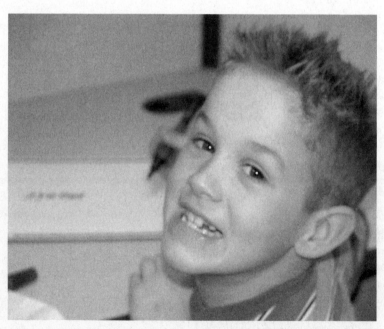

Portfolios allow a teacher to develop a picture of the whole student and chart his or her growth across time.

TYPES OF PORTFOLIOS

Just as there are several different kinds of assessment, there are also multiple types of portfolios. Each type of portfolio serves a different purpose in the process of assessment and instruction, and therefore contains varying artifacts.

Baseline Portfolios

Cohen and Wiener (2003) have written extensively on the portfolio process and have created a chronology for the development of a portfolio-based system of assessment and instruction. Their model begins with two baseline portfolios: (1) the teacher portfolio and (2) the student portfolio. The *baseline teacher portfolio* contains any diagnostic assessments, background information, observations, and anecdotal notes collected before and during the initial student conference. The *baseline student portfolio* is made up of student interest inventories and self-concept questionnaires, self-selected student work samples, and information obtained from the student's family. Together, the two portfolios serve as baseline data on the student's academic, social, and affective strengths and needs (Cohen & Wiener, 2003, p. 105).

Cumulative and Summative Portfolios

As the year progresses, the teacher and student each create what Cohen and Wiener (2003) call an "*ongoing cumulative portfolio*" (p. 105). This portfolio is formative in nature because it showcases a student's growth over time. *Formative assessments* have been defined as "a process that leads to decisions that occur during instruction, for the purpose of determining what adjustments to instruction should be made" (Mertler, 2003, p. 321). In this way, the cumulative portfolio serves as an ongoing collection of data that the student and teacher use to guide all instructional decisions. Cohen and Wiener (2003) suggest creating separate cumulative portfolios for the teacher and the student that will later be combined into the final or *summative portfolio*. The summative portfolio is meant to demonstrate overall growth across the school year and follow the student to the next grade level. If used properly, this portfolio will then serve as the baseline portfolio for the upcoming school year.

Grading and Report Cards

Even though portfolios are an excellent means of tracking a student's progress, all teachers are required to prepare report cards based on grades collected over the school year. Portfolios should contain pieces of work that are not only representative of progress across time but also support the grades earned by students. By having portfolio conferences with students, the teacher and student can review the contents of the portfolio, compare them against the grade-level grading criteria, and discuss the student's grades. Often, by discussing the criteria with the student, and then the parents, everyone will understand the progress made by the student toward meeting the grade-level standards and work together to develop a plan for improvement. These conferences also demonstrate the student's strengths as well with the supporting documentation. It is important to review the portfolio as a part of the report card/portfolio conference so that both parents and the student understand what went into the grade. According to Wiggins (1998), "a single grade often hides more than it reveals" (p. 248). He goes on to stress the importance of developing clear grading criteria so that the grade has more meaning and serves to guide teaching and learning. Ultimately, the grade should serve to "summarize students' school performance" (Wiggins, 1998, p. 247). Without the addition of a learning portfolio and a parent, student, and teacher conference, grades do little to clarify a student's strengths and needs.

PORTFOLIO AND REPORT CARD CONFERENCES: PARENTS, STUDENTS, AND TEACHERS

A key element of the portfolio process is the regular inclusion of student–teacher conferences. Without the reflective conferencing piece, a portfolio is nothing more than a work sample folder. It is important for the student and teacher to revisit the portfolios on a regular basis to adjust learning goals and instruction. To make the most of the conferencing time, teachers can develop a format for the conferences that can be taught to the students. In this way, both parties know the expectations for a conference prior to meeting.

Cohen and Wiener (2003) have created what they call *The Four Cs of Conferencing* (p. 204): (a) collecting, (b) collaborating, (c) consulting, and (d) communicating. They contend that in order to implement portfolio assessment successfully, all four components must be equally embraced.

The first C (*collection*) in the process involves the careful selection of artifacts to be reflected upon and added to the portfolio. The importance of the selection process cannot be stressed enough because the artifacts serve as the basis for the entire portfolio assessment process.

During the *collaborative* phase, students are taught to informally talk to one another, as well as to their parents and teacher, to discuss their progress. The continual feedback loop helps the students to engage in the learning process and take ownership of their education.

Intermixed within the collection of artifacts and the continual collaboration with others is the *consulting* aspect of portfolios. It is at this time that the conferencing portion becomes more formalized. A conferencing protocol may be developed and later incorporated into the student's portfolio along with feedback from the stakeholders involved in the process. It is here that parents are formally brought into the portfolio process. Together, the first three aspects are dependent on the fourth C, which is *communication*. Constant communication is essential to the process. It may be in oral or written form, in large or small groups, and it serves to facilitate the learning process.

By considering all of the people involved in the education of one child and opening up the lines of communication, ELLs can have successful, engaging, and lifelong learning experiences in school.

REVISITING THE *CHAPTER ANTICIPATION GUIDE:*

Spend a few minutes reviewing the statements presented in the Chapter Anticipation Guide at the beginning of the chapter. Compare your notes with those **highlighted**.

End-of-the-Chapter Anticipation Guide

Agree	Disagree	Statement
	✗	Student-led parent conferences work best when implemented after grade 3. *False—As was evidenced by the classroom vignette as the beginning of the chapter, student-led conferences can be used quite successfully as early as kindergarten if the students and teacher are well prepared. This preparation involves more than rehearsing the event; rather, it becomes an integral part of the classroom teaching and learning environment on a daily basis.*
✗		When bringing an interpreter to a conference, it is best to look at the parent rather than the interpreter during the conversation. *This is true! It is our natural tendency to want to look at the person who is speaking, which in this case is the interpreter, but we have to change our way of thinking in this type of situation. By looking at the interpreter, it leaves the parents out of the conversation taking place in regard to their own child. The message we unknowingly send to the parents is that we do not value their presence at the conference, and in turn, we do not value what they have to say because they do not speak English. This is a powerful message.*
	✗	When evaluating assessment results, it is most important to identify the student's areas of need. *False—While it is important to understand the student's areas of need, it is equally important to identify his or her strengths as well. By building upon these strengths, the student will grow exponentially in academic abilities. A valuable side effect of this growth is an increased level of confidence in his or her ability to learn.*

Agree	Disagree	Statement
	✗	It is unnecessary to maintain both formative and summative portfolios for ELLs and English-only students in the regular classroom. *False—Because formative and summative portfolios serve different purposes, they are both essential elements of a solid classroom assessment system. Formative portfolios are more fluid representations of a student's progress across the school year, while summative portfolios move with the student across his or her entire educational career and denote progress across years.*
✗		Developing assessment-based instructional goals allows teachers to provide relevant instruction on a daily basis. *True—This statement summarizes the main goal of this entire book. It shows the importance of providing ELLs with appropriate instruction based on sound assessment of their strengths and needs on a daily basis. While the book focuses on ELLs, this is an important goal for all learners if they are to make the maximum academic growth and develop a desire to become lifelong learners who are motivated and excited about learning.*

CHAPTER ELEVEN

Instructional Assessment in Practice: A Case Study

Read through each of the following statements prior to reading the chapter. Place a checkmark in either the box labeled "agree" or "disagree" depending on whether you believe the statement to be true or false. As you read the chapter, refer back to the chart and confirm or modify your initial responses.

Initial Chapter Anticipation Guide

Agree	Disagree	Statement
		A case study depends on a quantitative analysis of a student's academic needs.
		Case knowledge helps a teacher to apply the knowledge gleaned through the study of assessment and instructional strategies.
		A student's affective and academic needs should be considered when developing an instructional plan for the student.
		Two or three main learning goals should be developed during each grading period. These goals should focus on an ELL's oral and written language abilities before moving into the area of reading comprehension.
		ELLs would benefit from being involved in the development of their learning goals. This would enhance ownership in the learning process.

What Is a Case Study?

A case study is a qualitative and quantitative report detailing relevant data about a person, group of people, critical event, community, or program (Patton, 1978). Within the context of this text, a case study will refer to one specific learner and will provide the reader with a detailed academic, social, and familial background on a student in the fourth grade. By reviewing the case and answering specific questions, the reader will begin to understand the processes involved in diagnostic teaching. It is an individualized process that requires constant refinement and modification. The end result will be a more specific and meaningful academic experience for developing readers.

Frager (1994) found that using a case study approach to the teaching of reading results in teachers' developing "a bank of case knowledge" that can be utilized on a day-to-day basis as they make decisions within the classroom (p. 392). This bank of case knowledge allows teachers to quickly draw from knowledge as they are faced with varying academic situations requiring immediate attention. Without such a wealth of information, teachers are often left with only one or two options or choices and may not select the most appropriate one for the child.

Tom (1985) found that teachers who have been educated using the case study approach are more willing to reflect upon a particular teaching situation and consider alternate teaching methods. These alternatives may fall outside of the normal range of options, allowing for more flexibility in the classroom.

It has been argued that case studies need to be based on real-life situations in order to provide teachers, or other professionals, with rich learning experiences (Anderson & Armbruster, 1984, 1990).

The following box provides a mini case study or snapshot of a student named Abraham Morales. This vignette will be used to demonstrate the power of a case study methodology to the teaching of ELLs. It will allow you to make instructional decisions based on his academic performance as well as on his affective needs. Spend a few minutes reading about Abraham and form an overall picture of him as a learner. As you are reading, think about the academic information that is *missing* from the vignette as well. The missing information can be filled in as you assess Abraham in the classroom.

Based on what you have read, begin to create a list of Abraham's academic strengths and areas of need. When going through the case, you may want to consider the following areas:

1. Abraham's attitude toward reading, writing, and school in general.
2. Abraham's family and community support system.
3. Abraham's ability to decode a text and read with fluency in both English and Spanish.
4. Abraham's ability to comprehend what has been read in both languages.

CASE STUDY *VIGNETTE*

Abraham Morales is a 10.4-year-old fourth-grade student at Ellis Elementary School. Abraham has attended Ellis Elementary since the beginning of first grade when he first moved to the United States from Mexico. Abraham's primary language is Spanish, although he is developing fluency in speaking English as well. At the end of first grade, Abraham was retained because he was not reading at the appropriate grade level. His first-grade teacher also stated that he refused to speak in class.

Abraham lives in an apartment close to school with his mother, father, and 6-year-old sister Monica. According to his interest inventory and through observations of his classroom behavior, Abraham seems to have a positive attitude toward school and learning in general. He has stated that he does not spend much time reading at home; he prefers to spend his afternoons playing outside with his friends. Abraham particularly enjoys playing basketball and soccer, riding his bike, and playing video games with his friends. He also enjoys watching television and spending time with his family.

Abraham's fourth-grade classroom teacher, Mrs. Marcus, is unsure if Abraham's learning difficulties are related to language confusions. She feels that he is working at least two years below grade level in both reading and writing and is beginning to shut down when he is asked to read aloud in class. Abraham's mother has noticed that he reads very slowly and is unable to recall most of what he has read. When Abraham is read to, he is able to retell the main ideas in a logical sequence. Abraham struggles with spelling and writing, often spending 5 to 10 minutes writing one or two simple sentences.

5. Discrepancy between the Abraham's grade level and reading level in English and Spanish.

6. Abraham's ability to write with meaning, fluency, and spelling that does not inhibit the reader's ability to understand what has been written.

7. Abraham's successful use of reading and writing strategies when working independently in English and Spanish.

These statements can serve to guide you through the evaluation process by providing a focus for interpreting the background information and academic data being presented, as well as determining the assessments that still need to be done. Over the next few pages you will find results from various formal and informal assessments that have been administered since the start of school in August. Review this data and begin to form a picture of Abraham as a student.

FIGURE 11.1   Excerpt from Abraham's Writing Journal

September 28th

I hav wun frnd at skole. He is my best frnd. Hes nam is tony and I lik hem. We lik to rid biks at my hose.

Abraham's Assessment Results (so far!)

WRITTEN LANGUAGE

Mrs. Marcus begins each class session by asking the students to write for 15 minutes in their journals. They can use the prompt she has written on the board, or they may choose a topic of their own. Generally, Abraham writes to the prompt. The topic for this piece of writing was: "Write about your best friend. Why do you like this person? What do you do together when you are not at school?"

The writing sample in Figure 11.1 is reflective of the quality and quantity of writing produced by Abraham each day. This particular piece took 15 minutes to write. The date was provided for Abraham on the chalkboard.

WORD IDENTIFICATION AND COMPREHENSION

Abraham's English word identification and comprehension ability was assessed using an Informal Reading Inventory (IRI). Because Abraham entered school in the United States in first grade, his teacher decided not to test his native language reading ability. You will find data charts summarizing his English assessment results in Tables 11.1, 11.2, and 11.3, and 11.4.

TABLE 11.1   Abraham's English IRI Results: Summary Table I: Comprehension and Word Recognition Percentages Chart

Reading Level	*WR in Isolation	*WR in Context	Oral Comprehension	Silent Comprehension	Average Comprehension	Listening Comprehension
PP	100%	98%	80%	85%	82.5%	
P	90%	95%	75%	80%	77.5%	
1	80%	87%	60%	70%	65%	
2	65%			50%	50%	95%
3						90%
4						85%
5						75%

(*WR = word recognition)

Adapted from Burns & Roe, 2002

TABLE 11.2   Summary Table II: Miscue Analysis Chart

Miscues	Mispronunciations	Substitutions	Repetitions	Omissions	*TA	Reversals	Row Totals
Totals	11	5	0	9	3	0	28
Meaning Changed	8	3	0	3	0	0	14
Self-Corrects	0	0	0	1	0	0	1

* TA = Teacher assistance provided to decode the word

Adapted from Burns & Roe, 2002

TABLE 11.3   Summary Table III: Comprehension Question Error Analysis Chart

Question Type	Number of Questions	Number of Errors	Percentage of Errors
Main Idea	13	10	76%
Details	12	8	66%
Sequencing	9	6	66%
Cause & Effect	9	6	66%
Inference	11	4	36%
Vocabulary	11	11	100%
Totals	65	45	68%

Adapted from Burns & Roe, 2002

TABLE 11.4 **Responses on Graded Word Lists**

Preprimer Word List	Primer Word List	1ˢᵗ Grade Word List	2ⁿᵈ Grade Word List
is	got	going	*today*
the	sat	*said*	green
an	dad	milk	*night*
but	come	*store*	there
can	*they*	stop	*school*
sit	and	park	snow
do	make	drink	*drawer*
go	like	goat	*think*
mom	red	*left*	*marched*
may	*gate*	went	swing

Table Legend: Bold—correct *Bold/Italic*—incorrect

STOP AND RESPOND CASE STUDY QUESTIONS

Based on the results of the IRI, answer the following questions:

1. What is Abraham's independent reading level, his instructional reading level, and his frustration level?
2. Is he more proficient at decoding words when they are in the context of a paragraph or when they are presented in isolation? What does this mean instructionally?
3. What are Abraham's areas of strength and need in regard to word recognition?
4. What are Abraham's areas of strength and need in regard to comprehension?

When you have finished your analysis, continue reading through Abraham's assessment results.

THE OBSERVATION SURVEY

Select portions of *The Observation Survey* (Clay, 2002) were administered to Abraham beginning with the letter and letter sounds recognition task. Abraham easily distinguished all of the consonant sounds but had some difficulty correctly making the sounds of the short vowels. When given the phoneme sentence dictation task, Abraham again struggled with the vowel sounds but overall was able to correctly identify the consonant sounds. Figure 11.2 presents a copy of his sentence dictation results.

FIGURE 11.2   Sample of Abraham's Sentence Dictation Task

> I can se the red bot tat we ar go in to haf a rde in.
>
> (I can see the red boat that we are going to have a ride in.)

RECEPTIVE VOCABULARY

Abraham's receptive vocabulary level was assessed in both English and Spanish using the *PPVT-III* and *TVIP*, respectively. Abraham scored in the 7th stanine in English and in the 8th stanine in Spanish. Both sets of scores place him in the above average range for English and Spanish receptive vocabulary. This is an important finding because it confirms the results of the IRI in which he was able to comprehend reading materials on grade level when they were read to him. This definitely supports the notion that Abraham may be an auditory learner who, with the proper instruction, will be able to read, write, and speak in English at grade level. He has the capacity to learn and may be

When working with students, it is essential to establish a warm, safe learning environment prior to beginning the process of formal assessment.

hindered by language confusions. It may be important to conduct additional assessments in order to delve more deeply into Abraham's abilities before making any additional instructional decisions. This is a good point to begin brainstorming his strengths, needs, and the areas needing further investigation.

After creating your list of strengths and needs using a template similar to Table 11.5, begin to brainstorm several teaching strategies that you might want to implement when instructing Abraham. You may want to prioritize your list so that initially you are

TABLE 11.5   Preliminary Instructional Assessment Chart

Areas of Language Arts	Strength Domains	Need Domains	Instructional Implications (Strategies)
Receptive Vocabulary			
Expressive Vocabulary			
Concepts of Print			
Phonemic Awareness			
Phonics			
Reading Fluency			
Word Recognition (in context)			
Word Recognition (in isolation)			
Reading Comprehension—Narrative			
Reading Comprehension—Expository			
Spelling			
Written Language			

just focusing your instruction on two or three main areas or learning goals while building upon the strengths Abraham brings to the classroom.

Once you have created your list, compare it with the information listed in Table 11.6. Do you agree or disagree what is being suggested? Would you prioritize Abraham's goals differently? That's the wonderful part of teaching—there are many paths that will help a student, so feel free to implement a variety of teaching techniques.

TABLE 11.6   Abraham's Instructional Assessment Chart

Areas of Language Arts	Strength Domains	Need Domains	Instructional Implications (Strategies)
Receptive Vocabulary	Abraham scored above grade level on the *TVIP*, which shows that his Spanish language receptive vocabulary is very strong. He seems to be very good at understanding what he hears in English as well as evidenced by his above grade level score on the *PPVT-III*, which tests English language receptive vocabulary.		Abraham may be an auditory learner so it is important to build on this ability. Abraham would benefit from using such strategies as DLTA, LEA, DRTA, and other strategies based on oral language and listening skills. He would probably also benefit from being read to daily and also listening to books on tape.
Expressive Vocabulary			
Concepts of Print	Abraham has mastered the following concepts of print: directionality, tracking, use of picture clues to decode texts, and many letter-sound correspondences.		
Phonemic Awareness	Abraham has the ability to break most CVC words into their individual sounds.	Abraham has difficulty blending sounds together.	

(Continued)

TABLE 11.6   *(Continued)*

Areas of Language Arts	Strength Domains	Need Domains	Instructional Implications (Strategies)
Phonics	Abraham has mastered many consonant sounds in English.	Abraham does not understand many blends, digraphs, and long vowel sounds.	
Reading Fluency		Abraham reads without fluency in English and Spanish and is beginning to shut down when asked to read orally.	Use of choral reading, shared reading, and repeated readings to build his confidence when reading aloud.
Word Recognition (in context)		Abraham did not learn to read in Spanish beyond the first-grade level. He struggles with decoding and comprehension in Spanish and English.	
Word Recognition (in isolation)	Abraham can decode basic CVC words and other 2- or 3-letter words.	Abraham often makes up nonsense words when he doesn't know how to decode a word. This shows that he doesn't always read for meaning.	
Reading Comprehension—Narrative		Abraham's English reading comprehension may be hindered by his lack of fluency and a lack of comprehension strategies.	Build his comprehension through the use of comprehension strategies such as QAR, DLTA, and DRTA using books at his independent reading level. Teach these strategies to his mother so she can use them at home as well. Incorporate a daily program of rereading familiar books. This will build his fluency and comprehension.

TABLE 11.6 *(Continued)*

Areas of Language Arts	Strength Domains	Need Domains	Instructional Implications (Strategies)
Reading Comprehension— Expository	Abraham enjoys non-fiction or expository reading topics such as baseball, soccer (most sports), and video games.	Abraham's English reading comprehension may be hindered by his lack of fluency and a lack of comprehension strategies.	Abraham would benefit from a reading program that incorporates both expository and narrative texts. It would be important to engage him in high-interest, appropriately leveled books. It would also be useful to teach him the SQ3R strategy for comprehending expository texts.
Spelling	Abraham can spell basic CVC words but has difficulty with more complex words that contain silent letters, long vowels, or more than one syllable.	Abraham's spelling and writing are labored. He may be hindered by his inability to spell conventionally, which may be due to his low vocabulary, reading, and phonics abilities.	Begin a developmentally based spelling program.
Written Language	Abraham has a basic understanding of sentence structure. Abraham begins each sentence with a capital letter and ends each sentence with a period or question mark.	Abraham's sentences are somewhat immature and repetitive. He often starts a sentence with "the" or "I" and rarely stays on topic. He is often unable to read his own writing.	Incorporate the Language Experience Approach (LEA) into his writing program to build his confidence before transitioning him to shared and interactive writing.
Affective Components of Language Arts	Abraham has a positive attitude about school and wants to learn.	Even though Abraham does seem to enjoy school, he is beginning to experience a great deal of academic frustration, which is causing him to shut down.	Because he enjoys school, teach him to be a cross-age teacher to read to younger children. This will build confidence and fluency.
Familial Components of Language Arts	Abraham's mother is supportive of him and wants to help in any way possible.		

As you review your chart and the chart presented in the text, keep in mind that this is a just a preliminary strengths and needs chart. It will continue to develop as you continually assess and instruct Abraham throughout the school year. Completing the chart is just the first step toward providing meaningful instruction.

Case Study Debriefing

One of the main assets exhibited by Abraham is his desire to learn and his love of school. Even though school is difficult for him, he maintains a positive attitude toward learning. This is an area to encourage and build upon. Allowing Abraham to experience daily successes in school will further enhance his love of learning. The use of cross-age tutoring has been shown to provide benefits to both the teacher and the learner. Allowing Abraham to act as a reader for younger children will provide him with an authentic reason to read and reread books. It is through this rereading process that he will develop fluency and prosody, which in turn, will have a positive impact on his reading comprehension. This practice will also help him to develop his reading and writing vocabulary levels. Abraham should be encouraged to read aloud in both Spanish and English. Focusing on his primary language will serve to strengthen his literacy skills in English. Because Abraham's mother can speak English but does not read and write in English, Abraham could be encouraged to work with his mother in both languages. His mother has shown a desire to support Abraham with his schoolwork and would therefore be receptive to Abraham's desire to read to her.

As Abraham engages in daily reading of familiar books, it would be important to incorporate such comprehension strategies into his repertoire of strategies as the Directed Reading-Thinking Activity (DRTA), Directed Listening-Thinking Activity (DLTA), and the Question-Answer-Response (QAR) strategy. These strategies focus on the use of predictions and questions to gain meaning from a text. Abraham could be taught to use them when reading to his younger buddy. This will not only help his buddy but also serve to increase his comprehension as well. By being able to use these strategies and then to teach them to someone else, Abraham will be able to internalize what he has learned and generalize it to new books and new learning situations. It should also help Abraham to become more comfortable with his reading abilities so that he will not shut down when he is asked to read aloud in class. It should also be noted that Abraham should always have time to preread a text several times before being asked to read in front of a group. This will allow him to develop more self-confidence when reading orally.

Because Abraham has a strong support system at home, it might be useful to have Abraham, his mother, and his sister spend time reading together in the evenings. To improve his writing abilities, the family could also keep journals and write in them about their daily events before going to bed. It would be a nice way to share about the school day while also supporting Abraham's writing. By writing daily in a nonthreatening environment, Abraham may begin to experiment with new vocabulary and phonetic spelling. It should be stressed that the journals are for expressing ideas and building writing confidence. As time progresses, the family could begin to collect favorite stories and photos to document their lives. Journaling becomes an authentic learning activity with a great deal of value.

It is my hope that the case study has provided a quick look at the thinking processes involved in evaluating a student's strengths and needs from a more holistic viewpoint. It is this process that differentiates instructional assessment-based teaching from other forms of classroom instruction.

REVISITING THE *CHAPTER ANTICIPATION GUIDE*

Spend a few minutes reviewing the statements presented in the Chapter Anticipation Guide at the beginning of the chapter. Compare your notes with those **highlighted**.

End-of-the-Chapter Anticipation Guide

Agree	Disagree	Statement
	✘	A case study depends on a quantitative analysis of a student's academic needs. *False—A case study should contain both quantitative and qualitative data collected about a student. The combination of both data types helps the teacher to develop a complete picture of the student's strengths and needs.*
✘		Case knowledge helps a teacher to apply the knowledge gleaned through the study of assessment and instructional strategies. *Yes! Studying real case scenarios provides an opportunity to apply knowledge gleaned through texts.*
✘		A student's affective and academic strengths and needs should be considered when developing an instructional plan for the student. *True—When developing an instructional plan for a student, it is important to consider the affective strengths and needs. The affective components can greatly impact a student's ability to perform academically.*

Agree	Disagree	Statement
	✗	Two or three main learning goals should be developed during each grading period. These goals should focus on an ELL's oral and written language abilities before moving into the area of reading comprehension. *False—Each ELL should be assessed and evaluated on an individual basis in order to create the appropriate learning goals and locate the best teaching methods. Also, it is not necessary to ignore reading comprehension while a student is still working to master the conventions of the English language. Comprehension should always be emphasized.*
✗		ELLs would benefit from being involved in the development of their learning goals. This would enhance ownership in the learning process. *Absolutely! It is always beneficial to encourage students to collaboratively develop learning goals and monitor their own progress. It is an excellent way of engaging students in the learning process while building ownership and increasing their level of efficacy in the educational process.*

Running Record Sheet

Name: _____   Date: _____

School: _____   Recorder: _____

	Errors	*Error*	*Accuracy*	*Self-Correction*
	Running Words	*Ratio*	*Rate*	*Ratio*

1. Independent   _____   1: _____   _____ %   1: _____

Title: _____

2. Instructional   _____   1: _____   _____ %   1: _____

Title: _____

3. Frustration   _____   1: _____   _____ %   1: _____

Title: _____

Comments: _____

_____

_____

Page or Sentence	Title	E	SC	E MSV	SC MSV

Page or Sentence	Title	E	SC	E MSV	SC MSV

Source: Brantley, 2004; adapted from Clay, 1991

Narrative Story Retelling Assessment

Child's Name: _____ Age: _____

Name of Story: _____

Date: _____

How Story Was Read: **Orally**   **Silently**   **Read to Student**
(circle one)

Directions: Score each story element based on the child's retelling. Point values are included next to each element. The student will receive more points if the student directly states the answer within his or her retelling without being prompted.

P = Prompted Response   UP = Unprompted Response

A. Names main character [2 points unprompted (UP); 1 point prompted (P)]:

B. Names other important characters [2 points UP; 1 point P]:

C. Names setting [2 points UP; 1 point P]:

D. Includes important events in the story (All = 4 UP, Most = 3 UP, Few = 2 UP; 1 = P):

E. Problem is stated [2 points UP; 1 point P]:

F. Resolution is stated [2 points UP; 1 point P]:

G. Story is told in sequence (Yes = 3 UP, Partially = 2 UP; 1 point P]:

H. Concludes story [2 points UP; 1 point P]:

I. States story theme or moral [1 point P]:

Highest Score Possible: 20   Child's Score: _____

Comments: _____

_____

Source: Brantley, 2004

Proofreading Checklist

Questions to ask yourself: (Put a checkmark in the blank after you answer each question.)

_____ 1. Did I begin each sentence with a capital letter?

_____ 2. Did I write each sentence as a complete thought?

_____ 3. Did I spell the words correctly or circle those words that I need to look up in the dictionary?

_____ 4. Did I remember to vary how I begin each sentence so they don't all begin with the words *the, I,* and *then?*

_____ 5. Did I remember <u>not</u> to start my sentences with the word *and?*

_____ 6. Did I leave enough space between my words?

_____ 7. Is my writing neat enough so that someone else could read my writing?

_____ 8. Did I leave a one-inch margin on my paper?

_____ 9. Did I write my name and date on my paper?

_____ 10. Did I read my story to be sure it makes sense and then make changes as needed?

_____ 11. Did I give my paper to a buddy to read and response to before I turned it in to the teacher?

(Brantley, 2004)

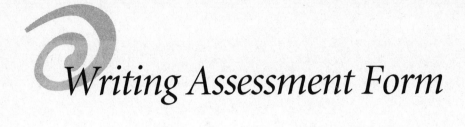

Writing Assessment Form

My Writing Reflections

Here are three things I like about my story:

1.

2.

3.

Here are three things I could do to make my story better:

1.

2.

3.

Buddy Response

This is what I liked best about your story:

Here are two questions I have for you:

It would make your story even better if you:

(Brantley, 2004)

Editor's Checklist for Expository Texts

Questions to ask yourself: (Put checkmark in the blank after you answer each question.)

_____ 1. Did I begin each sentence with a capital letter and end each with the appropriate punctuation mark?

_____ 2. Did I create a new paragraph for each new idea?

_____ 3. Did I indent each new paragraph?

_____ 4. Does each paragraph have a topic sentence and at least four supporting sentences?

_____ 5. Did I add a transitional sentence between one new idea and another?

_____ 6. Did I edit my writing to be sure it made sense and make any needed corrections?

_____ 7. Did I write a powerful opening statement that will grab the reader's attention?

_____ 8. Did I proofread my paper and correct my spelling errors?

9. **You are now ready to self-evaluate your composition and then have a peer evaluate it.**

(Brantley, 2004)

Assessment Recording Sheet

Name: _____ Grade Level: _____

Date	Assessment Administered	Child's Strengths/ Areas of Need	Instructional Recommendations
	<u>**Concepts of Print:**</u> An assessment that shows what a child knows about letters, sounds, words, directionality, picture cues, tracking, and punctuation.		
	Observation Survey: **Letter Identification:** A task used to determine if a child can name the upper- and lowercase letters of the alphabet and also distinguish the sound made by each letter.		
	Hearing Sounds in Words: A dictation task that requires the child to record a dictated sentence. The product is scored by counting the phonemes which are represented using letters.		
	Word Reading: A sight word reading assessment consisting of 15 high-frequency words. The child is scored for reading accuracy.		

Date	Assessment Administered	Child's Strengths/ Areas of Need	Instructional Recommendations
	Writing Vocabulary: An observational writing task in which a child is given 10 minutes to write down all of the words in his or her writing vocabulary. It is scored for accuracy of spelling.		
	Running Record: A systematic reading miscue assessment based on a 100-word passage from a leveled text. It is used to determine a child's use of reading strategies, the type and quality of miscues made when reading orally, and the correct level of text for independent and instructional reading.		
	Interest Inventory: An informal measure of a child's reading, writing, and personal interests. The results are used to help a teacher select high-interest texts and instructional materials and strategies.		
	Writing Sample: A writing sample, of varying genres, collected at various intervals throughout the 10-week tutoring period. The samples are scored using a rubric based on the six traits of writing as well as through writing conferences and self-reflection.		
	Jordan Left-Right Reversal Test: This quick test asks students to identify letters, numbers, and words (in and out of context) that contain some reversals to determine if the child can distinguish when they are reversed. It can indicate a vision or visual perception difficulty.		

References

Adams, M.J. (1991). Why not phonics and whole language? In O.J.L. Tzeng & H. Singer (Eds.). *Perception of print: Reading research in experimental psychology* (pp. 197–221). Hillsdale, NJ: Lawrence Erlbaum Associates.

Adams, M.J. (2001). Alphabetic anxiety and explicit, systematic phonics instruction: A cognitive science perspective. In S.B. Neuman & D.K. Dickinson (Eds.), *Handbook of early literacy research.* New York: Guilford Press.

Allington, R.L. (1995). *No quick fix: Rethinking literacy programs in America's elementary schools.* Newark, DE: International Reading Association.

Allington, R.L., & Cunningham, P.M. (2002). *Schools that work* (2nd ed.). New York: Longman.

Alvermann, D.E. (1991). The discussion web: A graphic aid for learning across the curriculum. *The Reading Teacher, 45,* 92–99.

Anderson, R.C., & Armbruster, B.B. (1990). Some maxims for learning and instruction. *Teachers College Record, 91(3),* 397–408.

Anderson, R.C. (1994). Role of the reader's schema in comprehension, learning, and memory. In R.B. Ruddell, M.R. Ruddell, & H. Singer (Eds.), *Theoretical models and processes of reading* (4th ed., pp. 469–482). Newark, DE: International Reading Association.

Anderson, T.H., & Armbruster, B.B. (1984). Studying. In P.D. Pearson, R. Barr, M.L. Kamil, & P. Mosenthal (Eds.), *Handbook of reading research* (pp. 657–679). New York: Longman.

Arter, J., & Spandel, V. (1992, Spring). Using portfolios of student work in instruction and assessment. *Educational Measurement: Issues and Practice,* 36–44.

Bear, D.R., Invernizzi, M., Templeton, S., & Johnston, F. (1996, 2004). *Words their way: Word study for phonics, vocabulary, and spelling instruction* (3rd ed.). Upper Saddle River, NJ: Merrill Prentice Hall.

Beers, J.W., & Henderson, E.H. (1977). A study of orthographic concepts among first graders. *Research in the Teaching of English, 3,* 133–148.

Bennett, M.J., & Bennett, J. (1996). *A developmental model of intercultural sensitivity: Language classroom applications.* Presentation, annual meeting, Teachers of English to Speakers of Other Languages. Chicago, IL.

Berger, L.R. (1996). Reader response journals: You make the meaning . . . and how. *Journal of Adolescent and Adult Literacy, 39,* 380–385.

Borich, G.D., & Tombari, M.L. (2004). *Educational assessment for the elementary and middle school classroom.* Upper Saddle River, NJ: Merrill Prentice Hall.

Brantley, D.K. (2004). *K–12 literacy assessments and strategies for instruction: A literacy tutoring handbook.* San Bernardino, CA: CSUSB Publications.

Brock, C.H., & Raphael, T.E. (2005). Whole group instruction: Unique challenges for English language learners. In *Windows to language, literacy and culture* (pp. 33–51). Newark, DE: International Reading Association.

Brown, A.L., Campione, J.C., & Day, J.D. (1981). Learning to read: On training students to learn from texts. *Educational Researcher, 10,* 14–21.

Brownell, R. (2000). *Expressive one-word picture vocabulary test.* Columbus, OH: Pearson Assessment Publications.

Bruner, J. (1975). Language as an instrument of thought. In A. Davies (Ed.), *Problems of language and learning.* London, England: Heinemann.

Burns, P.C., & Roe, B.D. (2002). *Informal reading inventory: Preprimer to twelfth grade.* (6th ed.) Boston: Houghton Mifflin.

Burns, P.C, Roe, B.D., & Ross, E.P. (1999). *Teaching reading in today's elementary schools.* Dallas, TX: Houghton Mifflin.

Calkins, L.M. (1986). *The art of teaching writing.* Portsmouth, NH: Heinemann.

Calkins, L.M. (1994). *The art of teaching writing (new edition).* Portsmouth, NH: Heinemann.

Campione, J. (1988). The basic structure of learning environments that fit the term *scaffold.* In C.B. Cazden (Ed.), *The language of discourse: The language of teaching and learning* (p. 104). Portsmouth, NH: Heinemann.

Canale, M. (1981). From communicative competence to communicative language pedagogy. In J. Richard & R. Schmidt (Eds.), *Language and communication.* New York: Longman.

Canale, M., & Swain, M. (1980). Theoretical bases of communicative approaches to second language teaching and testing. *Applied Linguistics, 1,* 1–47.

Chomsky, N. (1959). Review of B.F. Skinner's "Verbal behavior." *Language, 35,* 26–58.

Clark, E.V. (1993). *The lexicon in acquisition.* Cambridge, UK: Cambridge University Press.

Clay, M.M. (1972, 1985). *The early detection of reading difficulties: A diagnostic survey with recovery procedures.* Auckland, New Zealand: Heinemann.

Clay, M.M. (1991). *Becoming literate: The construction of inner control.* Portsmouth, NH: Heinemann.

Clay, M.M. (1993). *Reading recovery: A guidebook for teachers in training.* Portsmouth, NH: Heinemann.

Clay, M.M. (1997, 2002). *An observation survey of early literacy achievement.* Portsmouth, NH: Heinemann.

Cohen, J.H., & Wiener, R.B. (2003). *Literacy portfolios: Improving assessment, teaching and learning* (2nd ed). Upper Saddle River, NJ: Pearson/Merrill Prentice Hall.

Commander, N.E., & Smith, B.D. (1996). Learning logs: A tool for cognitive monitoring. *Journal of Adult and Adolescent Literacy, 39,* 446–453.

Cooter, R.B., & Thomas, M. (1998). *Venn diagram hula hoops.* Unpublished manuscript. Fort Worth, TX: Texas Christian University.

Cooter, R.B., Jr., & Flynt, E.S. (1996). *Teaching reading in the content areas.* Englewood Cliffs, NJ: Prentice Hall.

Crawford, A.N. (2005). Communicative approaches to second-language acquisition: The bridge to second-language literacy. In G.G. Garcia (Ed.), *English learners: Reaching the highest level of English literacy.* Upper Saddle River, NJ: Pearson/Merrill Prentice Hall.

Cummins, J. (1978). Educational implications of mother tongue maintenance in minority language groups. *The Canadian Modern Language Review, 34,* 395–416.

Cummins, J. (1981). The role of primary language development in promoting educational success for language minority students. *Schooling and language minority students: A theoretical framework.* Los Angeles, CA: Evaluation, Dissemination and Assessment Center, California State University, Los Angeles.

Cummins, J. (2005). Reading and the bilingual student: Fact and fiction. In G.G. Garcia (Ed.), *English learners: Reaching the highest level of English literacy.* Upper Saddle River, NJ: Pearson/Merrill Prentice Hall.

Cunningham, P.M. (1995). *Phonics they use: Words for reading and writing* (2nd ed.). New York: Harper Collins.

Deci, E.L., & Ryan, R.M. (1985). *Intrinsic motivation and self-determination in human behavior.* New York: Plenum.

Deci, E.L., & Ryan, R.M. (1987). The support of autonomy and the control of behavior. *Journal of Personality and School Psychology, 53,* 1024–1037.

Denzin, N.K., & Lincoln, Y.C. (1994). *Handbook of qualitative research.* Thousand Oaks, CA: Sage Publications.

Diaz, E., & Flores, B. (2001). Teachers as sociocultural, sociohistorical mediators. In M. de la Luz Reyes & J.J. Halcon (Eds.), *The best for our children: Critical perspectives on literacy for Latino students.* New York: Teachers College Press.

Díaz-Rico, L.T., & Weed, K.Z. (2002). *The crosscultural, language, academic development handbook: A complete K–12 reference guide.* Boston: Allyn and Bacon.

Diller, K. (1978). *The language teaching controversy.* Rowley, MA: Newbury House.

Dunn, L.M., & Dunn, L.M. (1997). *The Peabody picture vocabulary test–III.* Circle Pines, MN: AGS Publications.

Dunn, L.M., Lugo, D.E., Padilla, E.R., & Dunn, L.M. (1986). *Test de Vocabulario en Imagenes Peabody.* Circle Pines, MN: AGS Publications.

Durkin, D. (1995). *Language issues: Readings for teachers.* White Plains, NY: Longman.

Echevarria, J., & Short, D. (2002). The sheltered observation protocol (SIOP). *Using the SIOP Manual.* Long Beach, CA: Center for Applied Linguistics at California State University, Long Beach.

Ekwall, E.E., & Shanker, J.L. (2000). *Ekwall/Shanker reading inventory* (4th ed.). Boston: Allyn and Bacon.

Elkonin, D.B. (1973). Reading in the U.S.S.R. In J. Downing (Ed.), *Comparative reading* (pp. 551–579). New York: Macmillan.

Ellery, V. (2005). *Creating strategic readers: Techniques for developing competency in phonemic awareness, phonics, fluency, vocabulary, and comprehension.* Newark, DE: International Reading Association.

Elley, W.B. (1992). *How in the world do students read?* The Hague, Netherlands: The International Association for the Evaluation of Educational Achievement.

Fields, M.V., & Spangler, K.L. (2000). *Let's begin reading right* (4th ed.). Upper Saddle River, NJ: Merrill Prentice Hall.

Fountas, I.C., & Pinnell, G.S. (1996). *Guided reading: Good first teaching for all children.* Portsmouth, NH: Heinemann.

Fountas, I.C., & Pinnell, G.S. (2001). *Guiding readers and writers (grades 3–6): Teaching comprehension, genre, and content literacy.* Portsmouth, NH: Heinemann.

Frager, A.M. (1994). Developing case knowledge in reading education. *Journal of Reading, 37,* 392–398.

Frank, C. (1999). *Ethnographic eyes: A teacher's guide to classroom observation.* Portsmouth, NH: Heinemann.

Frayer, D., Frederick, W.C., & Klausmeir, H.J. (1969). *A schema for testing the level of concept mastery* (Working paper No. 16). Madison, WI: University of Wisconsin, Wisconsin Research and Development Center for Cognitive Learning.

Freeman, Y., & Freeman, D. (1998). *ESL/EFL teaching: Principles for practice.* Portsmouth, NH: Heinemann.

Freeman, Y., & Freeman, D. (2005). Teaching English learners to read: Learning or acquisition. In G.G. García (Ed.), *English learners: Reaching the highest level of English literacy.* Upper Saddle River, NJ: Pearson/Merrill Prentice Hall.

Gambrell, L.B., Pfeiffer, W., & Wilson, R. (1985). The effects of retelling upon reading comprehension and recall of text information. *Journal of Educational Research, 78,* 216–220.

García, G.G., & Beltrán, D. (2005). Revisioning the blueprint: Building for the academic success of English learners. In G.G. García (Ed.), *English learners: Reaching the highest level of English literacy.* Upper Saddle River, NJ: Pearson/Merrill Prentice Hall.

Gee, J.P. (1992). *The social mind: Language, ideology and social practice.* New York: Bergin and Garvey.

Gentry, J.R. (1981). Learning to spell developmentally. *The Reading Teacher, 34,* 378–381.

Golnick, D.M., & Chinn, P.C. (2002). *Multicultural education in a pluralistic society* (6th ed.). Upper Saddle River, NJ: Merrill Prentice Hall.

Goodman, K.S. (1986). *What's whole in whole language?* Richmond Hill, Ontario, Canada: Scholastic TAB Publications.

Goswami, U. (2000). Phonological and lexical processes. In M.L. Kamil, P.B. Mosenthal, P.D. Pearson, & R. Barr (Eds.), *Handbook of reading research* (vol. 3, pp. 251–267). Mahwah, NJ: Lawrence Erlbaum Associates.

Goswami, U. (2001). Early phonological development and the acquisition of literacy. In S.B. Neuman & D.K. Dickinson (Eds.), *Handbook of early literacy research.* New York: Guilford Press.

Gredler, M.E., & Johnson, R.L. (2004). *Assessment in the literacy classroom.* Boston: Allyn and Bacon.

Gunning, T.G. (2002). *Assessing and correcting reading difficulties.* Boston: Allyn and Bacon.

Halliday, M. (1975). *Learning how to mean: Explorations in the development of language.* London: Edward Arnold.

Hammill, D.D., & Larsen, S.D. (1996). *Test of written language-III.* Circle Pines, MN: AGS Publishing.

Heath, S.B. (1983). *Ways with words: Language, life and work in communities and classrooms.* New York: Cambridge University Press.

Henderson, E.H. (1990). *Teaching spelling.* Boston: Houghton Mifflin.

Herbert, R. (1979, 1983). *The basic inventory of natural language (BINL)*. San Bernardino, CA: CHECpoint Systems Inc.

Hiebert, E.H., Valencia, S.W., & Afflerbach, P.P. (1994). In S.W. Valencia, E.H. Hiebert, & P.P. Afflerbach (Eds.), *Authentic reading assessment: Practices and possibilities*. Newark, DE: International Reading Association.

Hoyt, L. (1998). *Revisit, reflect, retell*. Portsmouth, NH: Heinemann.

Hresko, W., Herron, S., & Peak, P. (1996). *Test of early written language-2*. Circle Pines, MN: AGS Publishing.

Hurley, S.R., & Tinajero, J.V. (2001). *Literacy assessment of second language learners*. Boston: Allyn and Bacon.

Hymes, D. (1961). The ethnography of speaking. In J. Pride & J. Holmes (Eds.), *Sociolinguistics*. Harmondsworth, UK: Penguin.

IDEA Language Proficiency Test. (2004). Brea, CA: Ballard & Tighe Publishers.

Johnson, D.D. (2001). *Vocabulary in the elementary and middle school*. Boston: Allyn and Bacon.

Johnston, P.H. (1997). *Knowing literacy: Constructive literacy assessment*. York, ME: Stenhouse Publishers.

Kaestle, C.F., Damon-Moore, H., Stedman, L.C., Tinsley, K., & Trollinger, W.V. (1991). *Literacy in the United States: Readers and reading since 1880*. New Haven, CN: Yale University Press.

Kottler, E., & Kottler, J.A. (2002). *Children with limited English* (2nd ed.). Thousand Oaks, CA: Corwin Press.

Krashen, S. (1981). *Second language acquisition and second language learning*. Oxford, UK: Pergamon.

Krashen, S. (1982). *Principles and practice in second language acquisition*. Oxford: Pergamon.

Krashen, S., & Terrell, T. (1983). *The natural approach: Language acquisition in the classroom*. Oxford, UK: Pergamon.

Lenski, S.D., & Nierstheimer, S.L. (2004). *Becoming a teacher of reading: A developmental approach*. Upper Saddle River, NJ: Merrill Prentice Hall.

Leont'ev, A.N. (1978). *Activity, consciousness, personality*. Englewood Cliffs, NJ: Prentice Hall.

Lindamood, C.H., & Lindamood, P.C. (1979). *The Lindamood auditory conceptualization (LAC) test*. Austin, TX: Pro-Ed.

Maxim, G.M. (1999). *Social studies and the elementary school child* (6th ed.). Upper Saddle River, NJ: Merrill Prentice Hall.

McLaughlin, B. (1987). *Theories of second language learning*. London, England: Arnold.

Mead, M. (1977). Anthropology and the climate of opinion. *Annals of New York Academy of Sciences, 293*, 1–11.

Mertler, C.A. (2003). *Classroom assessment: A practical guide for teachers*. Glendale, CA: Pyrczak.

Morrow, L.M. (1985). Retelling stories: A strategy for improving children's comprehension, concept of story structure and oral language complexity. *Elementary School Journal, 85*, 647–661.

Morrow, L.M. (2001). *Literacy development in the early years: Helping children read and write*. Boston: Allyn and Bacon.

Munõz-Sandoval, A.F., Cummins, J., Alvado, C.G., & Ruef, M.L. (1998). *The bilingual verbal abilities test.* Itasca, IL: Riverside Publishing.

Nagy, W.E., Herman, P.A., Anderson, R.C. (1985). Learning words from context. *Reading Research Quarterly, 20,* 172–193.

National Reading Panel (NRP). (2000). *Report of the National Reading Panel: Teaching children to read.* Washington, DC: National Institute of Child Health and Human Development.

Nessell, D.D. (1981). *The language experience approach to reading.* New York: Teachers College Press.

Nieto, S. (1992). *Affirming diversity: The sociopolitical context of multicultural education.* Boston: Pearson/Allyn and Bacon.

Nieto, S. (2004). *Affirming diversity: The sociopolitical context of multicultural education* (4th ed.). Boston: Pearson/Allyn and Bacon.

No Child Left Behind Act of 2001, Pub. L., No. 107–110, 115 Stat. 1425 (2002).

Nolen, S.B. (2003). Learning environment, achievement, and motivation in high school science. *Journal of Research in Science Teaching, 40,* 347–368.

Ogle, D. (1986). K-W-L: A teaching model that develops active reading of expository text. *The Reading Teacher, 39(6),* 564–570.

Oosterhof, A. (1999). *Developing and using classroom assessments* (2nd ed.). Upper Saddle River, NJ: Merrill.

Osbourne, J.W. (1997). Race and academic disidentification. *The Journal of Educational Psychology, 89,* 728–736.

Patton, M. (1978). *How to use qualitative methods in evaluation.* Newbury Park, CA: Sage Publishers.

Pearson, D. (2000). *What sorts of programs and practices are supported by research? A reading from the radical middle.* Ann Arbor, MI: CIERA.

Peregoy, S.F., & Boyle, O.F. (2005). English learners reading English: What we know, what we need to know. In Z. Fang (Ed.), *Literacy teaching and learning: Current issues and trends.* Upper Saddle River, NJ: Pearson/Merrill Prentice Hall.

Peregoy, S.F., & Boyle, O.F. (2001). *Reading, writing & learning in ESL: A resource book for K–12 teachers.* New York: Addison Wesley Longman.

Perfetti, C.A. (2005). Cognitive research can inform reading instruction. In Z. Fang (Ed.), *Literacy teaching and learning: Current issues and trends.* Upper Saddle River, NJ: Pearson/Merrill Prentice Hall.

Pikulski, J.J., & Chard, D.J. (2005). Fluency: Bridge between decoding and reading comprehension. *The Reading Teacher, 58,* 510–519.

Popham, W.J. (2001). *The truth about testing: An educator's call to action.* Alexandria, VA: Association of Supervision and Curriculum Development.

Raphael, T.E. (1984). Teaching learners about sources of information for answering comprehension questions. *Journal of Reading, 27,* 303–311.

Read, C. (1971). Pre-school children's knowledge of English phonology. *Harvard Educational Review, 41 (1),* 1–34.

Readence, J.E., Bean, T.W., & Baldwin, R.S. (1998). *Content area literacy* (6th ed.). Dubuque, IA: Kendall/Hunt.

Reutzel, R.B., & Cooter, D.R. (2003). *Strategies for reading assessment and instruction: Helping every child succeed.* Upper Saddle River, NJ: Merrill Prentice Hall.

Rumelhart, D.E. (1980). Schemata: The building blocks of cognition. In R.J. Shapiro, B.C. Bruce, & W.F. Brewer (Eds.), *Theoretical issues in reading comprehension* (pp. 38–58). Hillsdale, NJ: Lawrence Erlbaum Associates.

Ryan, R.M., Koestner, R., & Deci, E.L. (1991). Ego-involved persistence: When free-choice behavior is not instrinsically motivated. *Motivation and Emotion, 15,* 185–205.

Samuels, S.J. (2002). Reading fluency: Its development and assessment. In A.E. Farstrup & S.J. (Eds.), *What research has to say about reading instruction* (3rd ed., pp. 166–184). Newark, DE: International Reading Association.

Saville-Troike, M. (1978). *A guide to culture in the classroom.* Rosslyn, VA: National Clearinghouse for Bilingual Education.

Scupin, R. (2000). *Religion and culture: An anthropological focus.* Upper Saddle River, NJ: Prentice-Hall.

Shannon, P. (1992). *The struggle to continue: Progressive reading education in the United States.* Portsmouth, NH: Heinemann.

Shannon, P. (1994). Introduction. In R. Barasch & C. James (Eds.), *Beyond the monitor model.* Boston: Heinle and Heinle.

Sinatra, R. (1997). *Inner-city games CAMP-US: Literacy training manual.* New York: St. John's University.

Sinatra, R., Gemake, J., Wielan, O.P., & Sinatra, C. (1998). *Teaching learners to think, read, and write more effectively.* The 1998 ASCD Annual Conference (March 23, 1998). San Antonio, TX.

Skinner, B.F. (1957). *Verbal behavior.* New York: Appleton, Century, Crofts.

Smith, F.S. (1987). *Insult to intelligence.* New York: Arbor House.

Spandel, V. (2001). *Creating writers through 6-trait writing assessment and instruction* (3rd ed.). New York: Addison Wesley Longman.

Spradley, J.P. (1980). *Participant observation.* New York: Holt, Rinehart & Winston.

Stiggins, R.J. (2005). *Student-involved assessment for learning* (4th ed.). Columbus, OH: Merrill Prentice Hall.

Taylor, C.S., & Nolen, S.B. (2005). *Classroom assessment: Supporting teaching and learning in real classrooms.* Upper Saddle River, NJ: Merrill Prentice Hall.

Templeton, S., & Bear, D. (Eds.). (1992). *Development of orthographic knowledge and the foundations of literacy: A memorial festschrift for Edmund H. Henderson.* Hillsdale, NJ: Lawrence Erlbaum Associates.

Templeton, S., & Bear, D.R. (1992). *Development of orthographic knowledge and the foundations of literacy.* Mahwah, NJ: Erlbaum.

Terrell, T. (1977). A natural approach to second language acquisition. *Modern Language Journal, 61,* 325–337.

Terrell, T. (1981). The natural approach in bilingual education. *Schooling and language minority students: A theoretical framework.* Los Angeles, CA: Evaluation, Dissemination and Assessment Center, California State University, Los Angeles.

Thomas, W.P., & Collier, V. (1997). *School effectiveness for language minority students.* Washington, DC: National Clearinghouse for Bilingual Education.

Thorndike, R.M. (2005). *Measurement and evaluation in psychology and education.* Upper Saddle River, NJ: Merrill Prentice Hall.

Tinajero, J., & Schifini, A. (1997). *Into English! Level B, teacher's guide.* Carmel, CA: Hampton-Brown Books.

Tom, A.R. (1985). Inquiring into inquiry-oriented teacher education. *Journal of Teacher Education, 36,* 35–44.

Tompkins, G. (2001). *Literacy for the 21st century: A balanced approach.* Upper Saddle River, NJ: Merrill Prentice Hall.

Tompkins, G. (2006). *Literacy for the 21st century: A balanced approach* (2nd ed.). Upper Saddle River, NJ: Merrill Prentice Hall.

Torgesen, J.K., & Bryant, B.R. (1994). *Test of phonological awareness (TOPA).* Austin, TX: Pro-Ed.

U.S. Census Bureau. (2000). *Census 2000.* Retrieved December 15, 2005, from www.centstats.census.gov/data/us/01000.pdf

Vygotsky, L. (1962). *Theory and language.* Cambridge, MA: MIT University Press.

Vygotsky, L. (1978). *Mind in society.* Cambridge, MA: Harvard University Press.

Walker, B.J. (2000). *Diagnostic teaching of reading: Techniques for instruction and assessment.* Upper Saddle River, NJ: Merrill Prentice Hall.

Walker, B.J. (2005). *Techniques for reading assessment and instruction.* Upper Saddle River, NJ: Merrill Prentice Hall.

Watson, K.W., & Barker, L.L. (1995). *Listen up: Skills assessment.* San Fransisco, CA: Jossey-Bass.

Weaver, C. (1994). *Reading process and practice: From socio-psycholinguistics to whole language* (2nd ed.). Portsmouth, NH: Heinemann.

Wiggins, G. (1998). *Educative assessment: Designing assessments to inform and improve student performance.* San Fransisco, CA: Jossey-Bass.

Wiley, H.I., & Deno, S.L. (2005). Oral reading and maze measurements as predictors of success for English learners on a state standards assessment. *Journal of Remedial and Special Education, 26,* 207–225.

Williams, C., Tighe, S., Dalton, E., & Amori, B. (1991). *The idea oral proficiency test.* Brea, CA: Ballard & Tighe.

Wood, D., Bruner, J., & Ross, G. (1976). The role of tutoring in problem solving. *Journal of Psychology and Psychiatry, 17,* 89–100.

Yopp, H.K. (1992). Developing phonemic awareness in young children. *The Reading Teacher, 45*(9), 696–703.

Yopp, H.K. (1995). A test for assessing phonemic awareness in young children. *The Reading Teacher, 40,* 20–28.

Yopp, H.K., & Troyer, S. (1992). *Training phonemic awareness in young children.* Unpublished manuscript.

Zhao. (2002). NCLEA Newsbulletin.

Zwiers, J. (2004). *Building reading comprehension habits in grades 6–12: A toolkit of classroom activities.* Newark, DE: International Reading Association.

Author Index

Subject Index